CORONATION STREET

STREET

THE INSIDE STORY

CORONATION STREET

THE INSIDE STORY

BILL PODMORE
WITH PETER REECE

Macdonald

A Macdonald Book

Copyright © Bill Podmore and Peter Reece 1990

First published in Great Britain in 1990
by Macdonald & Co (Publishers) Ltd
London & Sydney

Unless otherwise stated, the photographs in this
book are the copyright © Granada Television.

British Library Cataloguing in Publication Data
Podmore, Bill
    Coronation Street. The Inside Story
    1. Television drama series in English
    I. Title   II. Reece, Peter
    791.45'5

    ISBN 0 356 17971 0

Reproduced, printed and bound in Great Britain by
BPCC Hazell Books Ltd
Member of BPCC Ltd
Aylesbury, Bucks, England

Typeset by 🅐 Tek Art Ltd, Croydon, Surrey

Macdonald & Co (Publishers) Ltd
Orbit House
1 New Fetter Lane
London EC4A 1AR

A member of Maxwell Macmillan Pergamon
Publishing Corporation

To Stan and Mabel

CONTENTS

1

STEPPING ON
TO THE STREET

The most successful show on television was tossed into my lap as a Christmas gift, and I nearly sent it back. It was a present so completely unexpected that the thought of just holding it in my hands filled me with an uncomfortable mixture of excitement and fear. I know the back of my neck was tingling and I suspect my knees were probably trembling in sympathy. But long before I dared to tear off the wrappings, I knew its acceptance would be one of the most important decisions I ever made in my life.

I was relaxing in my office at Granada's Manchester studios in December 1975, enjoying the satisfaction of having completed a second series of a situation comedy called My Brother's Keeper. For a while, there was nothing more to do than mind my own business and amuse myself with thoughts of persuading the powers which held the purse strings to lift a third series off the ground.

Telephones, of course, were invented to disturb such quiet moments of contentment, and resisting the overwhelming temptation to ignore it, I answered the call.

It came from 'upstairs', and as a rule those summons arrived with the ring of urgency. This invitation didn't quite seem to fit in that frame. David Plowright, who was then programme controller, asked me to his office for what his

secretary had beguilingly described as 'a chat about things'.

But as his diary seemed distinctly more ink-marked than mine, he didn't waste time on the pleasantries. With one simple, devastating sentence he turned my life upside down.

'Bill, I'd like you to take over as producer of Coronation Street.'

His tone somehow managed to fall between command and request. Later, I reflected that it may well have been the former masquerading as the latter, but at the time it left me far too stunned to reply.

Granada, like any organisation, great or small, has a well-oiled and efficient rumour machine, but for once its finely-tuned antennae had not even twitched. There hadn't been so much as a murmur. For the whole eavesdropping apparatus to have missed even a whisper on a change of this magnitude was unthinkable.

I remember trying to answer but the words were not forming, and when I finally spoke, the reply must have sounded remarkably trite. 'I don't think that's quite my cup of tea,' I stumbled, trying desperately to get my scrambled thoughts together with a measured evasion plan. I stared through the window across the cold grey cityscape and blindly searched rooftops for an avenue of escape.

Eventually I thought of what might pass as an excuse, and began rather lamely explaining that my roots were deep in comedy. It was an area of television production in which I felt happy and settled, and there were no evident parallels to be drawn with Coronation Street. The serial was recognised quite distinctly as a drama, and very much on the opposite side of my working fence.

David Plowright was a seasoned campaigner in such exchanges, and with a smile of victory already spreading across his face, he turned the argument to his advantage.

'Now that's why I think you would be absolutely right for the Street,' he countered with all the confidence of a man who knew he was about to score a major point. 'Maybe one of the things wrong with the programme is that it hasn't enough comedy content. I'd like you to take it over and put the zest back into it.'

I knew then I had lost the day, although my final agreement was short on enthusiasm. 'I don't want to do it,' I protested. 'But if you really are insisting, and you believe I can put it right, then I'll have a go.'

As a wild parting shot, I insisted my promise held good for one year only. But that, I strongly suspected, fell on deaf ears. Try as I might to grasp at what should have been an overwhelming sense of thrill, I wandered back to my office puzzling over what on earth I had allowed myself to be talked into and feeling, quite frankly, almost as bleak as the December weather.

The thought of being responsible for producing the longest running and most successful television drama series ever would have been daunting at any time. At that moment, approaching Christmas 1975, Coronation Street looked like a monster.

I was being let loose on a national institution and the responsibility weighed enormously. Coronation Street wasn't just another television show, it was a staggeringly successful organisation which had already influenced a generation, a major company in its own right, and I was being thrown into the managing director's chair.

My mind began to create visions of the fearsome creature rolling along week after week, year after year. The more imaginings I conjured up the less I liked them. There would be no more long weekends, no more time off unless the holidays were official, and certainly no more between-series breaks where I could sit back and muse pleasantly on what I might do next.

Every thought seemed to produce another burden. First, the show had to be bucked up. It had plunged from the number-one spot in the audience ratings, and recently had even managed to tumble alarmingly out of the top ten.

Then I had to face the Street's ten regular writers, probably the finest in the business, an awesome array of talent with years of experience. Les Duxbury and Adele Rose had been there almost from the beginning. Harry Kershaw, a lovely and intelligent man, a fine producer and an exceptional writer, had nursed the Street from its infancy. Meeting them was no great problem. The dark little fear which lurked in the recesses of my mind was that some of the show's faults might possibly lie at their door.

The first thing, of course, was to meet the cast. By now the rumour machine was in overdrive and Susi Hush, the outgoing producer, offered to take me down to the rehearsal room to introduce me officially.

As Susi and I walked towards the

The corner shop end of the original studio set

studio, I thought I might lighten the tension by asking if there were any perks that went with producing Coronation Street. Susi looked at me with a quizzical smile which seemed to imply that I didn't know what I was letting myself in for. She slowly shook her head.

Susi left the Street by mutual agreement. She handed me the reins without the slightest hint of animosity, or regret for that matter. In fact, Susi gave me the distinct impression that she was very relieved to unload the burden.

I had met most of the cast either as friends in the building or from the few occasions I had stepped in to direct the show. Even so, being introduced as the new boss held its anxieties. These turned out to be groundless. Everyone seemed pleased to see me.

A year earlier I had directed a couple of episodes in which Rita Fairclough was persuaded to pick up the threads of her cabaret singing career under the guidance of her new agent, the smarmy Alec Gilroy. A classic little line, delivered by Roy Barraclough with his perfect precision, had stuck in my memory. A London cabaret agent might have enquired about Rita's stage gowns. Not Alec Gilroy. He bluntly asked: 'How are yer for frocks, luv?'

Barbara Knox had paid me a lovely compliment, saying how much she'd enjoyed my direction and hoped I would eventually take over the show. I suspected others shared that wish and, although I was still very nervous, it was a great plus to know I was genuinely welcome.

The writers were no less generous in their greeting. We hit it off immediately. Coronation Street appeared to be limping along on a diet of heavy social comment or flighty romance, and everyone seemed to agree with my initial diagnosis that the show was suffering from a lack of laughter and fun.

Having agreed to give the Street my best shot, although perhaps only for a year, I had to study at least the more recent episodes. At that time I didn't even follow the serial. If I happened to be home at 7.30 on Monday or Wednesday evening I'd watch it, but you could hardly count me as a regular viewer.

I lost myself in videos for a few hours, and it didn't take long before I saw that there was little or no comedy left. Coronation Street had managed to lose its sense of humour, and I suspected I knew just where to find it. There were some wonderful characters: Hilda and Stan Ogden, Annie Walker and Bet Lynch, Ena Sharples and Minnie Caldwell, Rita Fairclough and Mavis Riley, Eddie Yeats, old Albert Tatlock – a host of people just waiting for funny situations.

I had learned all about laughter, and the tears that so often go with it, producing and directing a series called Nearest and Dearest. It was end-of-the-pier humour; good, honest, down-to-earth vulgarity and very funny on air. Backstage it was a different story. Its two stars, Hilda Baker and Jimmy Jewel, got on badly from the start, and by the end of three series they loathed each other.

Winning the first few laughs along Coronation Street was magically easy in comparison. Jimmy and Hilda were stand-up musical-hall comics whose prodigious natural talents made it difficult for them to accept the necessary direction for a carefully timed and presented television programme. Now, I had a cast of professional actors and actresses bursting with new enthusiasm to be told how the key elements of entertainment and comedy could be re-injected into their show.

Happily, time was on my side. Coronation Street is always planned three

The Street's biggest ever line-up; cast, writers and production crew celebrate the 2000th episode at Mottram Hall, Cheshire

months in advance and I inherited at least twenty-four scripts at various stages of writing and planning. That suited me fine. The programme couldn't and wouldn't be changed overnight. The new strands of humour I was encouraging the writers and artists to weave in had to come gently and naturally. The last thing I wanted was for viewers to sit bolt upright in their armchairs one Monday and say: 'What the hell's happened to Coronation Street?'

From pilot to producer of Britain's Number One soap opera – Bill Podmore

2

THE PILOT

My childhood was punctuated by endless waves of bombers. There were days when the sky appeared black with aircraft. First it was the Hampdens, then the Wellingtons and mighty Lancasters, heading from the airfields of Lincolnshire to blitz far-away places. I was eight years old when war broke out and as the conflict gathered pace, those aircraft meant only glamour and excitement. Death and destruction, or any thought for the aircrews who might never return, played no part in my schoolboy fantasy.

When aircraft didn't fill the sky, I filled my head with aeroplane books or magazines, and when my imagination wasn't in the clouds I would pack any spare space with jokes.

Jokes came secondary to planes, but only just. They fascinated me. I loved laughter and scoured the playground for funny stories to entertain the family. Pure schoolboy humour, I'm sure, but no one seemed to mind, least of all my dad, Stan.

He had a wonderful sense of humour and if these things can be handed down from father to son, I like to think that's where I acquired mine. Nothing ever seemed to depress Stan, and when he wasn't working as a butcher he indulged his other great love in life, fighting the Hun.

Dad thought the army life was wonderful. During the First World War he was assigned to the catering corps, but ran out of luck while scouring Flanders for supplies and got caught up in a mustard-gas raid. He painted vivid pictures of the bombing and described rivers of liquid gas flowing down the gutters. There was no escape and by the time he had managed to rejoin his unit he was blinded. Field hospitals were simply set up amid the stench and mud of the trenches, and for two weeks he bathed his eyes in liquid paraffin, not knowing whether he would ever see again. It must have been terrifying, but he told it like an adventure story.

Rats were his greatest horror. He could feel them running over his body, but couldn't see them coming. He laughed as he told the stories. Everyone else shivered. His sight never fully recovered and he wore glasses for the rest of his life.

A bullet in the knee finally forced him back to England, but not for long. He was assigned to a training camp which he claimed was so boring he volunteered to go back to the front line. When everyone else was desperate to get out of France, Stan Podmore insisted on going back.

By the time the Second World War came along he was too old for the call up. But to his delight an old mate suggested he volunteer for the artillery regiment and Dad was back in the uniform he loved. My mother, Mabel, couldn't make up her mind whether to be amazed or angry, but she was a wonderfully long-suffering lady, and she had no option but to let him go. For Dad, the call to arms must have been a double delight. This time he had a fresh outrage to avenge. A German bomber en route to Sheffield had been intercepted by a fighter and in its effort to escape had unloaded its bombs over our home town of Gainsborough. There were a number of casualties but in Father's eyes the most serious by far was the Peacock, his favourite pub.

I remember Father laughing as he told me about one of his postings – to an ack-ack gun guarding Woolwich Arsenal. One night there was an air raid and a bomb fell far too close for comfort. Dad was blown off his feet and landed somewhat painfully upside down on the lid of his tin helmet. From all accounts he was still chuckling when they carted him off for first aid. I suppose he was something of a nutcase, but when it came down to it he did more than his fair share of fighting for King and country.

He seemed to laugh at everything and encouraged me to do the same. At home I was the joker in the pack, the youngest of six, with three sisters and two brothers. Stan, named after the old man, was old enough to join the RAF before the war started; Peter later joined the Fleet Air Arm. I chose a technical education, joined the local air training corps, and the Royal Air Force seemed a natural career choice.

I considered the offer of an apprenticeship at Cranwell to study radio and radar a rather irksome road to fulfilling my ambition. But after three years of basic training I was accepted for aircrew training and offered an opportunity to win my pilot's wings.

Bill Podmore, the young pilot, in the cockpit of a Harvard (Photo: Bill Podmore)

At the age of twenty, I was posted to RAF Heaney, just outside Bulawayo in Rhodesia, for nine months' training. Apartheid sickened me, and I grew to dislike the white population. They treated the blacks abominably. I was then posted to Somerset, for conversion training to Meteor jet fighters, but again it wasn't a happy experience and during the course, in just over a week, two of my close friends were killed. One crashed in a Meteor over England, the other over Germany in a Venom.

I decided that my RAF career was to be neither long nor distinguished, and offered to resign my commission. My course work wasn't going well, and it was possibly only a question of time before they gave me the boot. The RAF had, however, spent five years training me at enormous expense and were justifiably angry when I decided to quit. Higher authority insisted that aptitude tests had at the outset marked me out as a navigator rather than a pilot, but I argued that I wasn't prepared to become a passenger, albeit a well-paid one.

As if to get my feet firmly back on the ground I took a temporary job as a farm labourer, but life on the land wasn't for me. There was work on offer with the naval radar department of the Marconi International Marine Division. The job specifications sounded grand, but in truth I was only marginally more qualified to carry them out than I was to build hayricks and harvest corn.

My brief was to order spares and find manufacturers of gunnery and radar location systems for three destroyers being built at Barrow in Furness for the Spanish navy. The Spaniards should be thankful they were not planning another Armada. I got thoroughly bored searching out former wartime equipment, which I suspected was almost obsolete, and trying to fit it into a modern warship. I reckon there are three destroyers still wandering the oceans of the world totally lost.

Finally I knocked at the door of the BBC. In 1954, the Beeb were feverishly overstaffing, knowing that in twelve months' time the first of the commercial TV stations would open and begin poaching staff. The only poaching ground was the BBC, and the corporation had to embark on a massive training programme if they were not eventually to leave themselves naked.

I was fortunate to be around at the right time, plus I had qualifications they thought suitable for work as a trainee cameraman. Within weeks I cut my teeth on a children's programme featuring Harry Corbett and his glove puppet, Sooty.

The aptitude required to be a pilot is not that far removed from the quick thinking and finely tuned eye and limb co-ordination needed to handle a television camera. Not that I was instantly handed one to play with. For the first weeks I hauled around armfuls of thick, black and very dirty camera cables.

Sooty seemed a far cry from the glamour of flying Meteor jets, but that didn't matter. This was show business. The atmosphere was electric. I was rubbing shoulders with the stars and television was a new and sparkling magic. Slowly I began to pick up the skills of camera work.

It wasn't long before the independent television companies came in search of staff. I shopped around for a promising niche, and was offered a three-year contract with ATV at almost double my BBC salary of £32 a month. Then, when the company secured a weekday franchise in the Midlands, I pioneered my way with promotion to the new Birmingham studios.

They were built inside an old cinema which nestled serenely between Ansells Brewery and a sauce factory on Aston Road North. The air was hardly alive with the sound of music, but between them the brewers and sauce-makers created some wonderful smells. Lunch was unnecessary. Breathing was a meal in itself.

In those days, television was terrific. They were great times filled with fun and excitement. It was all free and easy, and no one even thought about demarcation lines between different studio jobs. Everyone mucked in and did whatever was necessary to put the show on the air. Our daily magazine programme, Lunchbox, was live and often very hairy. If things went wrong they just had to be glossed over as best we could manage and on with the show.

I even used to appear as an extra, which I thoroughly enjoyed. I was a lot slimmer then, and wore a full beard. Lunchbox had a resident singer, David Galbraith, and one day the producer, Reg Watson (now king of soaps, including Neighbours, in Australia), decided to add a punchline to a song called 'You Stepped out of a Dream'. He persuaded me to dress up in a long evening gown and a blonde wig. As David sang, I was to sit with my back to camera, elegantly poised on a balustrade, for all the world like the lady of his dreams. As the final notes died away I turned to his outstretched arms and grinned inanely through my whiskers.

That kind of spur-of-the-moment, innovative fun soon went out of the window. The unions arrived hungry for power and did their best to wreck the pleasures which made the early days of television so exciting. Props workers squabbled with stage hands about who should move a chair two inches. If the director called for a simple alteration on the set the artist, or almost anyone else for that matter, wasn't allowed to touch it. Everything stopped while the appropriate union man came over and did it for them.

Television was changing rapidly and not all of it for the better. It was about this time that I set my sights on Manchester where the recently franchised Granada Television Company had set up shop.

3

FLYING HIGH IN LONDON AND MANCHESTER

Working with Reg Watson at Birmingham proved valuable experience, and his generous reference helped open the doors of Granada Television. The recently formed consortium was led by Sidney and Cecil Bernstein, brothers who had made their names in the cinema business.

They had won the independent television franchise for the north west of England after shrewd market research had identified it as a region with a large population driven indoors for long periods by heavy rain. The Bernsteins had found a rich field in which to sow the seeds of a mass television audience and time proved their judgement correct.

Although the company headquarters were in Manchester, the group recognised that the powerbase of show business was still entrenched in London. Many British film and theatre stars lived in or near the city, and it was a Mecca for international celebrities. To save on production and accommodation costs, Granada opened a light entertainment studio at the Chelsea Palace rather than bring everyone up to the North.

Originally I applied for a number two cameraman's job, a rank bestowed on me at Birmingham and a position I would have been quite happy to stick with for a while. But a particularly helpful Granada executive who interviewed me had other ideas. He evidently held an unshakeable belief that the only motive for a change of employer was promotion. After a lengthy interview during which we discussed the possibilities of me trying my hand at just about every job from production manager to programme director, I set off south with the high-flying title of senior cameraman. In two and a half years I had risen from raw trainee to the top job. Whether I was ever qualified to hold it down is anyone's guess, but in timescale terms, I suspect it stands as something of a record.

Television was still in its infancy, unsophisticated and packed with excitement. Everyone was beginning to recognise the enormous impact it would make on the entertainment industry, and at that moment London was the place to be. It was September 1957, the swinging sixties were just around the corner and the Chelsea Palace was fashionably central on the King's Road.

The studio was equipped with a Mole-Richardson camera crane – a massive picture-capturing machine with the camera bolted to a rotating platform at the end of a long metal boom. Counterbalanced at the opposite end by great slabs of lead, the camera could be swung up and down and from side to side with the grace of a ballerina. I had steered one of these monsters around a studio floor, but life at the sharp end was an electrifying experience.

It was one I had to come to terms with very swiftly. I was the new senior cameraman and this was to be my regular seat in the wondrous scheme of things.

The first ride to the studio roof was hair-raising enough. Vulnerably dependent on the skills of the operators below, I had a nagging suspicion that their competence might be as questionable as mine. Lift-off in the contraption was akin to the heart-stopping moment an aircraft lurches into the air, so that at least was not unfamiliar. But it was still deeply unnerving and, as the newly-appointed top gun, I couldn't allow the slightest suspicion to filter down to the studio floor that being swung around like a trapeze artist was other than second nature to me. The high-wire act became just another new skill to learn in those first heady days. The studio was a helter skelter of rehearsals and transmissions with very little time to spot the mistakes, deliberate or otherwise.

On Wednesday we produced Spot the Tune with Marion Ryan, and on Friday the studio was given over to The Army Game. But the highlight of the week was a spectacular hour-long entertainment show called 'Chelsea at Nine' which went out live on Tuesday nights.

Among its presenters were the giants of West End theatre and Hollywood – great names like Charles Laughton, Jack Hawkins, and Douglas Fairbanks Jr., stars who could attract guests from the world's stage.

Imagine Marlon Brando or Clint Eastwood suddenly popping up to stand in for Wogan. Our stars played host for up to four weeks at a time. But these were the late fifties, and television was flexing its muscles with sufficient power to make cinema moguls shake in their boots, and had enough cachet to pull its stars.

Many of the great pianists appeared on Chelsea at Nine – Julius Katchen, Poushinoff, and Cherkassky, together with violinists of the calibre of Yehudi Menuhin and Isaac Stern.

Maria Callas made her first television appearance on the programme and her reputation as the Tigress of La Scala spread terror throughout the studio. Such fears were unfounded. She charmed us, and it seemed to be mutual. Maria Callas may have thrown her tantrums in the great opera houses of the world, but in our studio she was the sweetest lady we could ever wish to meet.

Another guest unfamiliar with television was Poushinoff, the great exponent of Chopin. I hurried back from lunch to catch him in rehearsal, and listened spellbound. When he had finished the piece, I couldn't resist offering my congratulations. 'Mr Poushinoff, that was magic.'

That lovely old man looked up, eyed me curiously and replied: 'No! What you do is magic. I just play the piano.'

Oscar Peterson came with Ella Fitzgerald, but when I again dashed back from lunch early in the hope of catching their rehearsal, the studio was empty. I couldn't resist cheekily sitting down at the piano, if only to boast later that I once tickled the Peterson ivories.

I could just about play the tune of 'Evening Shadows Make Me Blue' with my right hand, while clumsily knocking out a bass beat with one finger on the left. It must have sounded painful. As I hammered away, I began to sense I wasn't alone.

I looked up and there stood the mighty figure of Oscar Peterson. I flushed with embarrassment, but he just smiled and said, 'Crazy man, just crazy.'

Jack Hawkins was another visitor who didn't care to stand on his superstar status. His idea of a good time was a couple of pints with the lads. We all adjourned one evening to our local, The Lord Nelson, where Jack's appearance caught the eye of an elderly man dressed like a solicitor's clerk.

Eventually the little man's curiosity got the better of him. In a well-rehearsed speech delivered in a voice clipped straight from the officers' mess, he introduced himself and told Jack how much he had enjoyed his films, in particular *Bridge on the River Kwai*.

Whether he caught Jack at the wrong moment, or whether the actor was simply feeling playful, I don't know, but he denied all knowledge of Jack Hawkins, assured him he was mistaken, and sent the disbelieving gentleman back to his seat looking puzzled and hurt.

He eyed us suspiciously from behind his pint until once again his curiosity overcame him. This time he insisted that from the manner, general bearing and voice in particular, he couldn't possibly have made a mistake in identifying Mr Jack Hawkins, the world-famous film actor.

Jack was warming to the game, and in a voice of mock threat said, 'I have told you once that I'm not Jack Hawkins. Now, how many more times do I have to tell you?'

It was a swift enough rebuff to send the intruder scuttling back to his corner where he nursed his smarting pride. Finally he got up to leave, and as he passed our group Jack, no doubt feeling pangs of remorse, stepped forward to reveal his identity.

'Just as you thought, sir, I am Jack Hawkins,' he admitted apologetically.

'Oh no you're not,' the man retorted.

'You can't be. Jack Hawkins is a gentleman.'

We all roared with laughter and Jack had to accept that the joke had rebounded on him.

In 1961, I was asked to take my camera crew from London to fill in for a period at the Manchester studios. The local elections were in full swing and their own cameramen were busy chasing around the hustings.

We were assigned to a relatively new programme; one we had barely heard of. It was called Coronation Street.

The show was but a few months old, and although it had made a spectacular impact on audiences in the regions where it was shown, it had failed to make any impression on myself or my crew. Perhaps we had been too busy with our own programmes to take much notice of Manchester's output, but more likely its transmission times on Friday and Monday evenings clashed with Nelson's call to do our duty at his bar. Although many of the Coronation Street stars were already household names, we could hardly put a name to a face.

In those days, the Friday programme was transmitted live, and the cast would go straight on to tele-record Monday's episode. Our instructions came down from the director on camera cards which, following the lines of the script, might say: 'Medium close up of Ken', or 'long shot over the shoulder of Ena and on to Annie serving Minnie in the snug'.

I'm sure the instructions would have been clear to the regular cameramen. It was just that my crew hadn't a clue who Ken was, or Minnie, or Annie.

The director was called down to make the necessary introductions. I remember Annie Walker standing as if rooted to the

Rovers' bar, her face a portrait of utter disbelief.

Then, on my behalf, one of the crew made the unforgivable mistake of asking someone to point out Ena. Just one glower from under that famous hairnet and the face of Ena Sharples was seared forever in my memory.

'Now look here, young man . . .'

4

SOBERING UP

Ena Sharples could make 'good morning' sound like a declaration of war. I've a sneaking suspicion that's exactly the way the old tartar meant it when we came face to face for a second time.

Almost seven years after that first stroll along the most famous street in the world, I was invited, as a newly qualified programme director, to cut my chattering teeth on Coronation Street.

Although thrilled to be assigned to the programme, I was understandably nervous of telling the most adored group of artists in Britain that for six months they would be taking their orders from me.

What little courage I managed to muster that December morning in 1967 evaporated at the rehearsal room door. Violet Carson, that lovely lady they called the Duchess, had undergone a chameleon-quick transformation, and was waiting as Ena with a nagging old score still to be settled with the uppity incomer from the London studio.

She gleefully sensed my fear. Flint-faced and steel-eyed, Coronation Street's matriarch, who could send milk sour at a glance, strode across the floor to greet me.

'Hello, Bill. Welcome. My train leaves at five-thirty.'

She smiled quietly at her victory, her eyes twinkling with pleasure, while I, rather timidly, attempted to laugh in defeat.

Ena Sharples, the old battle-axe, had cut me down to size; but at that moment the ice cracked. A handshake sealed the beginning of a good friendship, and a lasting mutual respect.

Granada's policy of allowing inexperienced directors to practise on the nation's number one programme is not quite as mystifying as might at first appear. With very few exceptions, the cast of Coronation Street fit snugly into their characters, and can often work with the minimum of direction. To some extent this frees the trainee to concentrate more on technical difficulties, which inevitably crop up as a programme is made. The series is thus a far gentler training ground than the assault course another programme might be. I was taking full advantage of this, but I was just the latest in a long line of new brooms to sweep the cobbles of Coronation Street. It would have been surprising if Violet Carson had been the only old hand wanting to test the quality of my bristles.

Some of the studio crew had a go next. They plastered the walls of the corner shop with little signs offering tins of cut-price peaches at 1/6d in the hope I might not notice. It was all harmless fun which helped to break the tension in the control room.

Then something happened which made everyone catch their breath. I

Jerry and Len in the Rovers

suspected Graham Haberfield, who played Len Fairclough's sidekick Jerry Booth, was also trying to send me up.

The scene was the Rovers bar. The script called for the pair to rehearse a bit of lively banter on the pitfalls of Christmas pudding making, but from my seat in the control room things sounded very odd. Either the microphones were faulty, or Jerry's words were decidedly slurred.

I stopped the rehearsal and told everyone how much I'd enjoyed the joke. Time was always the last thing we dared waste, and I wanted to get on with the job. Then the studio floor manager whispered into a microphone, 'Bill, he's not sending you up. He's drunk.'

I couldn't believe it. Day one, and I had a crisis. Harry Kershaw was producer at the time and I telephoned his office where, thank goodness, he had been watching the performance on a monitor.

'Send him home,' was Harry's terse solution. But when I relayed this to the studio floor, Graham shouted back, 'Tell him to bloody well come down here and tell me himself.'

I was so furious I might have done just that, and Mr Haberfield might have left the studio sadder and wiser. Graham, however, decided that discretion was the better part of valour, and beat a hasty retreat. The following morning he was soberly ashamed and pouring out profuse apologies.

It would have been impossible not to have forgiven him. Graham was one of the gentlest people I have ever met. He was incapable of hurting a fly, not an ounce of badness in him, and true to his promise he never again allowed drink to interfere with an episode which I directed.

A few days later, at a Christmas party

at Pat Phoenix's home, he introduced me to his wife Valerie, saying: 'This is Bill Podmore, the man who was so kind to me after I made such an exhibition of myself in the studio.' It was very touching.

That little terraced backstreet, sandwiched between Rosamund Street and the viaduct, is not quite as cosy as many of its millions of fans might imagine. Over the years the real life tragedies have often eclipsed those played out in front of the cameras, and Peter Adamson was the first serious casualty.

Peter had been hitting the bottle for years, trying, as he explained later, to escape his fame, the taxman and sorrow for his wife, Jean, who was bravely battling her way through a life of almost constant pain as arthritis slowly crippled her. He was devoted to her, but by the time I was called in to direct Coronation Street, he was a very heavy drinker.

One week, the crucial story-line centred around Len Fairclough winning a plumbing contract for the flats which were being constructed on the site of Ena's recently demolished Glad Tidings Mission. The incurably workshy Stan Ogden was called in to help Len until the rest of the flats' workforce discovered he was anything but a card-carrying member of their normally watertight union, and downed tools in protest.

The strike stopped the job, and a showdown between the belligerent Councillor Fairclough and the union's local representative was scheduled for high noon in the bar of the Rovers. It was to be the climax of the story, a very important scene and Peter, true to recent form, was drunk. In fact he was so sloshed he had the greatest difficulty in delivering his lines at all.

This wasn't a rehearsal which could be abandoned, like the Graham Haberfield drama, until the actor had sobered up. It was recording day. The camera crews, lighting technicians, sound men, actors, extras and Uncle Tom Cobley were waiting to shoot the scene. We had no alternative but to struggle on.

Peter didn't look too bad in the wide-angle shots, where the camera was peering over the shoulders of the assembled strikers and into the arena of the bar where the two were supposed to be squaring up to each other. He was just swaying gently backwards and forwards; with a little clever camera work we might have got away with that.

But in close-up we could never hide a face which looked leeringly on the wrong side of a bottle of scotch. Peter could hardly speak, never mind put up a convincing argument, which made it impossible for his sparring partner in the verbal battle to play his part either. Without crisp timing, the whole scene fell apart.

We shot as much as we could and then set a bleak and unique precedent for Coronation Street. For the first time in circumstances other than a complete technical breakdown, we had to go back into studio the following week, position all the actors and extras on exactly the same spots as before, re-shoot the close-ups, and tape the words of a thankfully sober Peter Adamson.

With a little help from the backroom boys in the video editing suite, we stitched the tape clips together, and somehow conjured up the latest in a long line of Len Fairclough cover-ups. It must have looked a lot better than I anticipated. Doris Speed telephoned with a welcome pat on the back: 'What a wonderful piece of surgery, dear boy.'

Peter had been pretty tipsy on set

many times before but we had always got away with it and I don't think a single viewer ever suspected. If they did, they let it pass. Harry Kershaw was not prepared to be so generous this time. For him it was the last straw. He had finally tired of firing warnings and rockets at Peter in an effort to bring his drinking habits under some semblance of control. It was time for action. The punishment had already been decided and given the green light at the highest management level. It was simply a question of how and when it was to be meted out to avoid throwing the whole of Coronation Street into chaos.

Harry was livid, but cunning enough to control his anger. Had he kicked Peter through the door at that moment, as he was sorely tempted to do, it would have meant throwing away the next three months' story-lines, many already plotted in detail, some even committed to script. Len Fairclough was a major figure, and woven into so many story plots his instant loss would have been too great an upset. Harry cleverly and quite correctly waited until every card could be played to the programme's advantage and then broke the news to Adamson that he would be suspended without pay in three months' time.

Peter was left in no doubt that his suspension would last for at least thirteen weeks, but the eventual length of the punishment would very much depend on his behaviour in the run-up period. As a gesture of good will, and there was precious little left by this time, Granada offered to foot any bills if Peter sought professional medical help to dry out.

The news rocked him. Peter had always gambled that the Street could never afford to lose him, even for a short while, simply because story-lines were plotted so far in advance. But this time Harry was holding all the aces. He had completely outwitted the actor and Peter slunk along to my office. Not only was he feeling very sorry for himself, but he was also tearfully pleading that he faced the loss of everything he had worked for, his lovely home and all the trappings fame had brought him.

He had come in search of sympathy, but I was as angry as anyone and there was none on offer. I told him I had always believed we were good mates, and that I thought he had let me down badly. I could say nothing to console Peter, other than to remind him that he had three months' grace to consider his future, plus all the help and support he needed to beat the bottle. It was not within my gift as director even to try to alter the suspension decision, supposing for one moment I could be persuaded to.

Peter needed to be punished, and harshly, if only to shock him into realising how very serious his drinking had become. It wasn't just his own life he was wrecking. His wife and two young sons were suffering terribly too.

Peter had drunkenly argued and occasionally brawled his way from pubs in the centre of Manchester to any which would entertain him on his way home to Bury. It had been tolerated far too long. The public did not differentiate between Peter Adamson and Len Fairclough, and Peter was getting into far deeper trouble than his television character ever did. There had been more cover-ups, official and unofficial, than anyone cared to count. They had to stop.

Drink was consuming Peter's life. He had reached the stage where each morning his first glimpse of daylight was through the bottom of a glass. It had long since passed the point where anyone could reason with him. He knew full

Peter Adamson – he beat the bottle

well the state he was in, but any mention of it only made him angry.

One morning Violet Carson came to me, complaining quietly and with great dignity, 'Bill, I really don't like working with people who have had too much to drink.'

She politely omitted to mention Peter's name but I knew whom she was talking about. I discreetly called Peter over to say I wouldn't be getting to his scenes for over an hour, and suggested he might head along to the canteen and have some coffee. I was being as gentle as possible, but that was not how he read the message; he squared up to me, shouting, 'Don't bloody patronise me!'

Peter obviously felt deeply guilty about his drunkenness. It was hopelessly beyond his control but he still couldn't come to terms with the thought that anyone else recognised the state he was in. For long enough he had tried to hide his level of addiction, and out of loyalty, misguided or not, the cast, the crew and everyone involved in the programme had at some time joined in the foolish charade.

Suspending Peter, even for a short length of time, was a hell of a decision to have to make. Len Fairclough was hugely popular, a bedrock character. Like so many of the original team, the choice of Peter Adamson had been a masterpiece of casting.

Peter had a great rugged quality, the right face and exactly the right build. His toughness only gave more weight to his acting skills. Off the set he could be as abrasive as the man he played, it was an underlying part of his nature which he passed on to Len. He turned him into a wonderfully earthy character who didn't mince words but was never unattractive to the legions of fans.

As long as he looked OK on the screen, and viewers didn't spot the truth, his drink problem was tolerated. But now, the whole show was in jeopardy, and Harry Kershaw's plan was backed by everyone to the highest level within Granada. It was exactly right, proof of which came six months later.

Peter Adamson beat the bottle at his first serious attempt and I admired him for it. The cast were delighted. The Len Fairclough of old was back and in wonderful shape. For him, drink really was the devil's work and with a fervour that bordered on evangelism he devoted a great deal of his spare time saving others from their personal hells. He did some wonderful work too. I know he was grateful that life had given him a second chance and he wanted to repay the debt.

I have heard it argued that the potential to become an alcoholic is present in some people from birth, a built-in self-destruct button just waiting to be pressed. For anyone with that potential, acting, offering as it does security one minute, the dole queue the next, is a dangerous profession.

Peter joined Alcoholics Anonymous and crusaded for them inside and outside the studios. He was by no means the only one at Granada with a drink problem and I know of quite a few people he went on to help.

Some years later, the Street had a visiting actor who had assured everyone that his notorious booze problems were behind him. At the crucial moment the truth was discovered and I know Peter went to his hotel to talk him through it. It was a typical caring gesture.

5

THE PROBLEM POTMAN

The producer of Coronation Street traditionally inherits the largest desk in the Granada Television empire and early in the new year of 1976, its custody was handed over to my somewhat reluctant hands. Whether the vast expanse of leather-topped wood and steel is a measure of the value placed on Britain's favourite soap, or merely an indication of the weight of problems and paperwork it must endure, I have never worked out.

Once behind that desk, I began a detailed survey of the Street, seeking the areas crying out for a facelift or even a face change. I had in mind redecoration

Bill Podmore behind the famous desk

rather than demolition, but then I spotted cracks in the corner shop which could never be papered over.

The community centre, the Rovers, the corner shop, the Kabin, Mike Baldwin's factory; more recently the café; these have been and are the focal points of community life. Perhaps they are not the birthplace of every story-line, but they are certainly the meeting places where gossip begins and the dramas take shape.

The corner shop, where Coronation Street's creator Tony Warren set the opening moments of the series in December 1960, had lost a good deal of its character. I suspected the weakness lay in the rather foolish decision to leave its day-to-day running in the hands of two young girls – Gail Potter and Tricia Hopkins. Youngsters have always played an important role in the Street's life, but without a more mature shop staff, the nitty gritty of conversation and tittle-tattle were never going to bounce around its walls.

I could see a tremendous future for Helen Worth, who played Gail, and decided to move her in as a lodger with Elsie Tanner. But sadly, Kathy Jones, who played Tricia, was to be my first casualty. Lovely as she was, Tricia didn't appear to me to be a natural Street character, and at a rather tearful meeting I broke the news to Kathy that she was to be written out of the show. I knew just where to find the more mature personality I believed should replace her.

I had been enormously impressed by an actress called Madge Hindle, who had played Lily in Nearest and Dearest, and decided to bring her in as Rene Bradshaw, the new shop owner. That left the little matter of finding her a husband, and if ever I saw a Mr Green the Grocer waiting to be cast, it had to be Alf Roberts.

Several things intrigued me about the mysterious Alf; how, for instance, had he managed to wander down Coronation Street in the first place? He didn't live there, and apart from his job at the local post office plus his work as a councillor, his only place in Weatherfield affairs appeared to be supping pints in the Rovers. But what really fascinated me was why on earth he chose to sup them wearing a ridiculous black bowler hat. We struck a deal. Alf could stay on the condition that he wed the lovely Rene, but the hat had to go.

That left one more nagging problem. Since the death of dear old Arthur Leslie in 1970, the bar of the Rovers had been dominated by women. Annie Walker, Jack's widow, had bravely soldiered on alone, but with Betty Turpin and a little later Bet Lynch, the ladies had ruled the roost for five years – a situation I was determined to change. A working-class, backstreet pub without a man on the scene didn't seem credible to me.

When it was decided that the Rovers should at least have a 'potman' helper to bring some balance to the sexes, Fred Feast appeared so perfect for the part, we didn't even bother to change his Christian name. Fred had originally driven into the Street back in 1970 as a bit-part baker's roundsman, and in the intervening years I had watched him capture some splendid cameo roles on television, and stored his name away as a future Coronation Street character.

His career was chequered to say the least. He was an ex-parachute instructor who landed on his feet when he auditioned on impulse at London's Windmill Theatre and was given a job as a stand-up comic working alongside the then almost unknown Bruce Forsyth. But from there on success seemed to have slipped through Fred's fingers like the sands of his native Scarborough. Pork butcher; proud owner of a trawler called the *Fidelity*; driving instructor, carpet salesman, publican, night-club owner and even compère of a performing dolphin show – Fred Feast had tried his hand at them all.

It was once said rather unkindly that potato-faced Fred looked like a heart attack searching for somewhere to happen. No one should have been fooled by his paunchy frame. Fred was a giant of a man, a one-time keep fit fanatic and feared sergeant in the RAF Parachute Regiment.

One of his proud boasts was that he trained Alan Ladd for his role in *The Red Beret*, although some say this amounted to no more than instructing the actor to abseil down the roof of a Ringway Airport hangar. Another boast, which endeared him to no one in Granada, was that twelve sparrows could perch on a certain part of his anatomy. His only gesture to modesty was to add that the last little bird would have to stand on one leg. Despite all this, he made the most wonderful job of creating the bumbling, bashful and much bullied Fred; the anti-hero we wanted, who won a huge army of fans.

It is a pity he didn't make any serious efforts to win a few more friends in the cast. Fred Gee had secured his place in the hearts of the nation, but I have to admit that as Fred Feast he was not the most popular of men on or off the set.

Fred enjoyed some rather vulgar habits which didn't go down well with the more serene, mature ladies of the Street. He wasn't averse to burping in a highly audible fashion, nor disinclined to breaking wind in every direction. He was, shall we say, earthy. Personally, I could forgive him almost everything because he was wonderful value playing Fred, and if you didn't mind the wind instruments he was quite entertaining off-stage.

Fred's trouble was that he never knew when to stop. There was a growing number of complaints of his behaviour in public. He was a regular visitor to what seemed a host of suburban pubs, accompanied by Gerry his 'minder', driver and drinking companion.

Most people who resemble a famous face usually manage to turn the situation to some degree of advantage. Not so a Manchester factory worker who bore the most remarkable resemblance to Fred. Had we ever needed a stand-in or someone to perform a double act, Vic Stevenson would have been the man to turn to. Not only did they share the same looks, right down to their choice in spectacle frames, their gestures were similar too. The pair might have passed for identical twins, although any such suggestion made Vic's blood run cold.

This quiet family man's problems started when he was chased around his local Woolworth's by a giggling group of girls demanding his autograph. That was when he realised he was Fred Feast's double, and from then on life became more and more difficult for the unfortunate fellow.

'I know Fred is a bit of a buffoon on screen, but what the man has done to deserve the stick I take, I can't imagine,' Vic complained bitterly. 'It seems everyone wants to have a go at him. The trouble is, they are taking it out on the wrong man.'

It reached a stage where hardly a day went by without someone reminding Vic of the haunting shadow of Fred. He lived what he called a waking nightmare for more than a year until he appealed to a Sunday newspaper to publish his picture and heartrending story in an effort to end his troubles.

Often, people had turned nasty when Vic refused to sign autographs on behalf of his lookalike. His explanations of mistaken identity were rarely accepted; people assumed it was Fred, who couldn't be bothered to sign his name. Vic wanted nothing more than a quiet life; he especially wanted to be able to drop into his local pubs for a quiet pint. I had every sympathy when I discovered that for no other reason than his resemblance to our star, he had been punched, kicked, banned from certain hostelries and had even had his car vandalised.

Fred gave us all more than our share of trouble. He was not much of an ambassador for Coronation Street and there were several occasions when I hauled him into the office for a dressing down. He would stand there like some great naughty schoolboy, looking full of remorse, although I doubt whether he ever was. Those reprimands didn't appear to mend his ways much.

On one particularly embarrassing occasion he distinguished himself at a Variety Club dinner by shaking bottles of champagne and spraying anyone within range. He might have thought that sort of childish behaviour very funny, but I was furious when the complaints came back.

He let us down so many times. One evening the manager of a well-known Manchester steak restaurant quietly took me on one side and said, 'I really don't like to complain about your artists, but I have to say something about the conduct of Fred Feast.'

Inwardly I groaned. I could imagine what was coming.

'He's been pretty objectionable,' the manager continued. 'Although it is nice to have stars in the restaurant, Fred takes terrible advantage of it.'

Fred had apparently developed a habit of wolfing down his steak almost to the last mouthful, then complaining volubly and refusing to pay. The manager had allowed Fred to get away with it to avoid further embarrassment. It was, of course, Fred taking advantage of his star status; he wanted something for nothing, and quite mistakenly thought that he should have been given free meals in the first place.

My offence was to forgive so often. Some of Fred's more outrageous exploits came back to me on the grapevine, some through blazing press headlines. These stories always had to be divided in two for a kick-off and it was never easy to discover the truth when headlines were pushed under my nose with the demand, 'What are you going to do about that?'

Fred was not one of nature's gentlemen, nor was he the greatest actor in the world. Nevertheless, I would have found it hard to replace him. He stood there and played himself, more or less. But in a programme like Coronation Street that is often the hallmark of success and we did have some wonderful fun out of him. John Stevenson wrote a marvellous sketch where Fred decided to change his image with a wig. Everyone in the Rovers had a go at him. When Annie Walker joined in you couldn't help feeling sorry for the great helpless buffoon.

Perhaps the way we handled the character turned him into something of a Jekyll and Hyde. In the Rovers he was always the underdog, constantly chided by Annie and wonderfully put down the moment he made any advance towards Bet Lynch. That may be the reason he felt he had to play such a swaggering, uncouth, almost bullying character in real life.

At one stage when Fred was obviously

Fred admires his far from fetching topknot

under strain and quite ill we wrote him out for a while. He took a much needed break and came back hoping for a gentle reintroduction to the programme. Instead he was greeted by heavy story-lines, which I should have noticed and called a halt to when the scripts were being prepared. By the time Fred came back and I realised he was facing quite a burden, it was too late for changes to be made.

One day we met in the street near to the studios and it was obvious that Fred was genuinely upset and worried about his workload. He said he was having the utmost difficulty coping with it. I couldn't work out why, and wondered whether he had personal problems on his mind. All I could promise was to make his life much easier as new scripts were planned. But before I could fulfil the pledge, Fred had decided to quit.

It had reached that time of the year when I had to start thinking about the annual renewals of the cast's contracts. This had to be considered well in advance, because of our advance planning schedule. We had no intention of getting rid of Fred. He was far too valuable as a character, despite the aggravation outside the studio, and his understandable wish for an easier time in the programme. As he had mentioned nothing about leaving, I assumed he wanted to stay, and prepared his contract for renewal.

Eventually he came to see me and announced in a rather cold, matter-of-fact manner: 'I'll not be signing on again.'

'I'm very upset to hear that,' I replied. 'But if that is your final decision and I can do nothing to change it, I hope you'll give us a few weeks to develop a strong story-line to take care of your exit.'

The story schedules were full, and there wasn't room to fit in another. I asked Fred to extend his current contract by a few weeks, possibly only three, to help us out.

His answer was an emphatic no, to which he added, 'My contract ends on November sixteenth and that's when I'm going.'

'I think that's more than a bit unreasonable considering all we have done for you, Fred,' I protested. 'Coronation Street has given you a golden opportunity. You're a household name and we made that for you. Surely you have some loyalty to us?'

'Why?' said he bluntly. At that I lost all patience with the man. Just as bluntly I said: 'All right, then you'll be written out with a whimper rather than a good dramatic exit.'

I was furious that anyone from the cast could be so pig-headed. I thought there must be a reason for his obstinacy, but I couldn't see it. Fred went, and a week or so later revealed all in a newspaper.

He slagged off the cast and saved a few vitriolic words for me. It upset everyone. That was only to be expected, but the majority eventually took the view, 'What else did we expect from the man?'

In his newspaper story, Fred complained that the pressure of learning scripts had become so intolerable he was having regular nightmares and fits of uncontrollable tears. If so, I think he might have had the courtesy to tell me

as producer. Had I had the slightest suspicion that his workload was damaging his health, steps would have been taken immediately to end the pressure and get him medical help.

Fred appeared in one or two productions, including a summer show in Jersey where he managed to fall out with his co-star, Rodney Bewes of The Likely Lads. Eventually Fred left the show, complaining once again that he was ill.

I have a good friend in Jersey, and often take my two children over there for a summer break. On one such occasion a couple of years back I'd heard that Fred had been seen on the island.

On our second morning we were in St Helier, and I said to the children, 'If you spot Fred before I do, give me a nudge and we'll dodge into a doorway.' We walked ten yards and turned to cross the road. A very recognisable voice boomed out, 'Bill!'

I turned round and there was Fred. I could only brave it out. We exchanged pleasantries, and then as bold as brass he asked, 'When am I coming back then?'

'Where to?' I asked, puzzled.

'To the Street,' said Fred.

'Never,' said I.

'Well that's straight enough,' he said. 'Cheerio.'

As far as I was concerned Fred had long since cooked his Coronation Street goose. As a character he was a serious loss, but the Street always survives. That is the marvellous thing about it; the programme is far bigger than any single person in it.

Now we have the wonderful Jack Duckworth in the bar and that's even better. He's a lovely man to work with, a total professional. There's no trouble, no nonsense, and he gives us everything we had in the Fred Gee character and much, much more.

6

'CATHERINE OF ALL THE BLEEDIN' RUSSIAS'

It was always immensely difficult to decipher the fine line which separated Pat Phoenix from Elsie Tanner. If there were two separate characters in the beginning, over the years the two had become so inextricably intertwined that I suspect Pat herself had problems identifying the fact from the fiction.

Pat was a star in every sense, and never passed up a chance to throw every

The Queen of the Soaps, with Bill Podmore

ounce of energy into living up to the image. She was flamboyant, loud and loving, a throwback to the magnificent mink-bikini days of Hollywood; an actress in a time-warp where the guiding light was the glitz and glamour of show-biz. She loved it.

Pat would arrive at the humblest rehearsal looking like a million dollars, and when it was over Coronation Street's Scarlett O'Hara swept out of the studio as if the streets of Manchester were the set of *Gone with the Wind*.

Seeing her wrapped in her beloved furs, Tony Warren would greet her, shouting, 'Here she comes. Catherine of all the bleedin' Russias.' It was a compliment she loved, and the one she quoted most.

Pat always saw herself as a star and worked very hard, with the help of some diligent press relations, to make very sure the status was accorded to Miss Phoenix and not Elsie Tanner.

She was probably the first member of the cast to be widely and equally known by both her real and stage names. But although the fans adored her, there were many in the cast, and others behind the show's scenes, who saw her natural flamboyance as an unharnessed arrogance which occasionally trod on everyone's toes.

For thirteen years, from earliest Street days, a succession of scriptwriters, directors and producers had fought to win control of Elsie Tanner's wardrobe, and finally declared it a glorious failure. Pat had become a law unto herself in make-up, hairstyling, and whatever she chose to wear. She had set out to shape Elsie Tanner into a screen legend, and in her book, legends never wore old coats and curlers.

In March 1973, the alarmed residents of Coronation Street were evacuated in a gas-leak drama. Albert Tatlock had been rushed to hospital after being overcome by fumes when Jerry Booth had attempted to take out the pensioner's ageing gas cooker and install a new electric one in its place.

The script called for Elsie to be half-way through washing her hair when the gas board pressed the panic button and the whole Street was evacuated to the Community Centre. The cast and production team expected Elsie to arrive breathless with her flame-red hair hanging lank and wet around her shoulders and shampoo bubbles in her ears. Not a chance! Pat swept on to the set, her hair neatly swathed in a sparkling white towelling turban, proudly making her entrance with all the grace of the Queen of Sheba.

The early arrival of a boyfriend called, on another occasion, for Elsie to be caught with her curlers in. It was explicitly scripted that her head should be covered in rollers. But that was not for the glamour-puss of Weatherfield. Somehow, Pat had managed to skate around the director's instructions with two tiny clips strategically placed in an otherwise perfect bouffant hairstyle. The First Lady of Soap placed her own loose interpretation on such matters and she was rarely challenged.

Two years before I took over the production chair, Pat had rather sensationally quit the show saying she was finally bored out of her brains having to turn up every day and wait hour after hour to deliver perhaps four lines. She had concluded that Elsie Tanner, sexpot of the sixties and self-styled Queen of the Soaps, had been reduced by the writers to a worn-out old has-been waiting for her bus pass and pension. It was high time, according to the Phoenix, that the lady spread her wings.

Pat's sadness, and often bitterness, about the neglect of her character went far back. When the programme celebrated its tenth anniversary, I happened to have been called in to direct a pair of episodes. ITN News were invited to film us in rehearsal, and before their camera crew arrived, Pat had been sounding off that all the fire and guts had been written out of Elsie.

She seemed particularly unhappy that day, and was loudly complaining that the few trite lines she had been given had little to do with Elsie, and could have been delivered by anyone without a soul noticing the difference. June Howson was producing at the time, and although she wasn't prepared to change the script, she came down to the rehearsal room and did what she could to appease Pat.

Quite suddenly, however, Sandra Gough, who played Irma Barlow, was taken ill, which called for a quick rejigging of the schedule. Instead of altering the script, Sandra's lines were handed out for other characters to deliver. The story remained the same; it was just that characters other than Sandra told it.

Pat seized on the moment. 'You see what I mean,' she declared. 'The scripts are so weak, any character can say anyone else's lines, and not only does no one notice, nobody even cares.'

Thank heavens the ITN cameras were not rolling at the time. Pat had been handed a golden opportunity to underline her point, and I could only throw up my hands and claim it was an emergency.

She was genuinely worried that the very heart of Elsie's character was being whittled away. Pat longed for a return to the original abrasive and gutsy Elsie, whose plump and bosomy Italian-style sex-symbol figure was so fashionable in the early sixties.

Unfortunately, since then Pat had done little to help herself. By this time, she had completely glamorised herself out of the original Elsie mould, and was so busy blaming the scriptwriters she failed even to suspect that she might be the prime cause of her own downfall.

It was becoming more and more difficult to create and write scenes which would portray the Elsie of old. Pat was never happy unless she was playing the Irish red-head, flaring with pride and anger. She hated having to stand in the shop to deliver a couple of innocuous lines. She firmly believed that if she was to be used at all, her character should be exploited to the full; she never came to terms with the fact that in a community such as Coronation Street, people do drop in at the shop or the pub with only 'hello' to say, or perhaps a couple of lines to add to the general conversation.

One character cannot carry a complete story and hope to make it credible. Other people have their story-lines passing through the programme, and they need the support of other members of the cast to pull the whole thing together. Pat seemed deludedly convinced that she could completely disappear from the scene if she wasn't right at the centre of the drama. She could never accept that every once in a while, in company with every other major Street character, she was required to play one of the highest-paid extras in show-business.

Pat left the Street for the first time in October 1973 in the company of Alan Browning, the actor she fell in love with and married after he had been brought in to play her screen husband. Together they took a play called *Gaslight* on a forty-three-week tour, but in the second year of the split with her beloved Elsie, I suspect work in the theatre had become harder to find, and with the money running out Pat was longing once again for the fame and cash of Coronation Street.

Her letter appealing for a second chance arrived almost exactly when I took over as producer and, as the decision was mine alone, I decided the comeback would be on terms I laid down. I had always been extremely fond of Pat and, with Susi Hush, I arranged to meet her for lunch at Manchester's Midland Hotel.

Pat didn't look at all well. Her nerves appeared to be stretched on a rack and, in her anxiety, I suspected she might have agreed to any proposal as long as it secured her place back in the programme. I had decided before the lunch that the only undertaking I needed before a deal could be struck was a solemn promise that the Elsie Tanner image would be a little more malleable. I steered the conversation around to the delicate subject of Elsie's dress sense.

'There has always been a big problem with the way you overdress, and so often dress out of character,' I explained, as gently as I could.

So far so good, at least there were no lunch plates flying.

'If we are to recreate the gritty and earthy character of the Elsie Tanner of old, then there must be some big changes to the way you used to look. For instance, if the script states you have just got out of bed, that's exactly how you should look. You don't come downstairs first thing looking as if you had just stepped out of the hairdresser's, and a damn good one at that.'

There was no argument; Pat listened carefully. My sermon over, she looked suitably contrite and made all the promises I needed to invite her back. I was delighted to welcome her, although

some in the cast were anything but happy. Pat had been away for two years, but for some, memories of the way she queened it as the Street's number one star were only too fresh in their minds.

Jean Alexander and Pat never hit it off. There was always friction between them, perhaps because their personalities were so contrasting. Pat would never miss the chance to play the big star, something that was very foreign to Jean's nature. She was as reserved as Pat was brash. But Jean was such a brilliant actress she didn't need to go around proving anything to anyone.

In 1968 there was a mistake in the timing of an episode in which Stan and Hilda were saying tearful farewells to their daughter Irma, emigrating to Australia with her husband, David.

In those days the show had to run to an exact twenty-five-and-a-half minutes, and we were something like forty-five seconds short. I was directing, and to fill in the gap I suggested a little scene where Mum and Dad went to the Rovers for a consolatory drink.

Extra lines were quickly written and I was crouched on the rehearsal room floor looking up at Hilda and Stan to give them some direction as they memorised the new script. Half-way through, we heard the click, click, click of high-heeled shoes. Without a word of apology or even an 'excuse me', Pat Phoenix marched between myself and the two artists, oblivious of the sin she had committed.

Jean was furious. At heart, Pat Phoenix was one of the kindest, most thoughtful and generous people I have ever met. But on the odd, quite infuriating occasion, of which that was a classic example, Pat would have her head in the clouds, indifferent to whatever was going on around her. To a stranger, it

Jean Alexander and Pat Phoenix never hit it off; Hilda and Elsie certainly had their moments

might have been mistaken for arrogance.

It was a side to her character I hoped I might attempt to change on her return, along with her wardrobe and make-up. I knew it would be at least three months before I began the rebuilding work. Stories were projected too far in advance to allow Elsie Tanner to slip back unnoticed. By the time she returned the programme had undergone dramatic changes.

I was beginning to weave some of my own ideas into the show. There was a fresh wave of enthusiasm sweeping the studio and we were beginning to see changes in places and faces. Although I

had the greatest affection and friendship for Pat, I had not the slightest doubt that she believed our eventual climb back to the top of the ratings was all due to her return to Elsie's old home at number eleven. To top it off nicely, she instantly forgot all her promises.

Some of her first scenes were shot on location away from the studio and, more important to Pat, away from my immediate supervision; I had no reason to be there for the filming. True to her old form, Pat arrived looking as though she had just stepped out of a Paris fashion house in a very smart designer-label raincoat.

Our wardrobe lady was the first to spot that Elsie's dress sense had gone way up-market yet again, and as politely as possible, reminded Pat, 'I don't think Bill will be happy with that coat. It looks far too expensive.'

But of course Pat had her grand entrance plotted to the last detail. 'It will be far too late before he gets round to noticing,' she explained. 'The raincoat will have been established on film and for the sake of continuity, Bill will have to allow me to wear it when I walk into the Rovers.'

Infuriatingly, the plan worked. I could have done nothing, except insist on the whole expensive business of reshooting her homecoming, and Pat even had her excuses rehearsed: 'The way I look and dress gives hope to all those millions of women out there of my age.'

She believed it implicitly. The one question she hadn't perhaps considered was whether her fans could afford to emulate her. Nevertheless, she had won her first point and would win many more before she quit for a second time, some years later, saying she was once again tired of Elsie Tanner.

Although Pat came back to the Street, her husband never joined her. One evening I called at their home in Hollingworth and, over a couple of drinks, Alan Browning raised the question. It would have been unfair to beat about the bush. I explained I had no plans to bring him back, and the subject was never mentioned again.

Pat and Alan drifted apart; mainly, I suspect, due to Alan's heavy drinking. In 1978 he died of liver failure. It was very sad, because he really was a skilful actor. If he hadn't taken such solace in the bottle, Alan's future in television and the theatre was assured.

Pat didn't even show up at his funeral. Publicly she announced she was staying in Devon to share her grief with close friends. The facts are easier to believe. Pat had recently undergone a facelift operation and couldn't possibly meet her public, even at her husband's funeral, looking anything less than perfect. Alan Browning had died at an inopportune moment. Pat's face was bruised.

At the service, just as Alan's coffin was sliding out of sight, the person next to me whispered, 'It's just as well Pat isn't here.' Even at that solemn moment I had to ask, 'Why?' 'Well,' came the reply, 'she would only have come dressed as Widow Twankey.' Cruel humour, but oh so true.

7

THE KILLING
OF ERNIE BISHOP

The killing of Ernie Bishop was an extraordinary affair. It exploded in my face, and the newspaper headlines, and somewhat soured the celebrations of my second anniversary in the driving seat of Coronation Street.

The story began straightforwardly enough when actor Stephen Hancock who played perhaps the most unlikely character to champion any cause, threatened to quit the show to safeguard a principle. But then, as so often happens in Coronation Street, the facts became thoroughly mixed up with fiction. By the time this complicated tale reached its bloody climax, I had been branded a contract killer, half Britain hated me, and the press had nicknamed me 'the Godfather'.

I have always considered it a great compliment that countless fans choose to believe that the lives of everyone in Coronation Street are as real as their own. But even acknowledging that has never quite prepared me for the overwhelming sadness so many seem to feel when a fictitious character dies on screen.

In any terraced backstreet the sudden loss of a well-loved personality is distressing. But when death's winged chariot clatters down Coronation Street, the whole nation mourns. On the night I arranged for poor Ernie Bishop to be brutally gunned down in a bungled wages snatch, the cries of anguish could be heard across the length and breadth of Britain.

Granada's switchboard was jammed by angry and grieving callers, letters of protest arrived by the sackload, the lobby against TV violence threw in their pennyworth, and one of Britain's finest documentary film makers, Norman Swallow, was so fascinated by events that he devoted half an hour of a series called This England to the tear-stained aftermath. Who could have guessed that the inoffensive soul of Ernie Bishop had found a place in so many people's affections?

The killing wasn't planned to distress the nation. In fact it wasn't planned at all. The popular myth is that Granada killed off Ernie either out of spite, or as a warning to others, because Stephen Hancock dared, like Oliver, to ask for more. Cash certainly played a prominent role in the affair but the size of Stephen's own pay cheque was not in question. The true story is a lot more complicated.

My office door was rarely shut. The accepted method of entry was to put your head round and see if I was free. The tone of the opening words decided whether the door should be closed on the conversation which followed.

From the moment Stephen entered I sensed it was something serious. He seemed so troubled, I thought he must be ill, or about to face serious surgery.

When he explained that he wanted to talk about his contract, I almost breathed a sigh of relief, and waited to hear what the problem might be.

What he actually said left me flabbergasted.

'I will not be signing mine because, in principle, I don't think the contracts are fair,' he began, and went on to explain in some detail why his beliefs left him little alternative but to say goodbye, after ten years.

Stephen admitted that he was happy enough with his pay cheque, but he thought it grossly unfair that members of the cast benefited from a variety of differing contracts guaranteeing the number of episodes in which they could appear.

Every actor and actress contracted to the Street was then – as now – guaranteed appearances in at least fifty-two episodes and paid accordingly. As there is also an unwritten rule which requires everyone to make themselves available for both episodes in any week, the contract has the effect of assuring them all of at least twenty-six weeks' work in any year. Just a few held contracts which, for varying reasons, promised them even more appearances.

However, since the earliest days of transmission, there existed a handful of people, including Pat Phoenix, Doris Speed and Peter Adamson, who were guaranteed payment for every one of the year's one hundred and four episodes. It didn't necessarily double their pay packets, but these were obviously fatter and the artists were never, of course, called upon to work the full fifty-two weeks a year.

Stephen insisted this wasn't fair and seemed determined to resign if the whole system of contracts wasn't brought into line. There was a measure of logic in his argument, and in an ideal world we might have gone to work to iron out the anomalies, and placed everyone on an equal footing. Perhaps the system wasn't scrupulously fair, but these things rarely are.

Although I had certain sympathies with Stephen's thoughts, I believed the distribution of episodes had been evaluated correctly according to input or the character's importance. There had been no other complaints on these grounds and I didn't form the impression that Stephen was complaining on behalf of any group of disgruntled artists, large or small.

In the final analysis, I wasn't prepared to change a complex and well-established system for the sake of one unhappy actor, and told him so. I also made it plain that I thought he was in danger of cutting off his nose to spite his face, and pleaded with him to go away and think long and hard about the salary and security he would be giving up if he left.

In fact we had three meetings to discuss the matter, with days rather than hours in between. This was to be no hurried decision. Each time, I asked Stephen to reconsider, hoping he would change his mind. Above all, I wanted to be absolutely sure he had all the time he needed to reach a decision. There was no hurry. He first came to see me long before his contract was due to be signed.

He bravely stuck by his beliefs and left no room for compromise. But if he could stick to his principles, then I felt thoroughly justified standing by mine, and with the impasse fully understood, Stephen left me no alternative but to write Ernie Bishop out of the show.

That might sound simple enough, but in fact it gave us yet another headache.

The shooting of Ernie Bishop

Ernie and Emily Bishop's marriage was made in heaven. He was a lay preacher and they looked to be the happiest and certainly the securest couple in the whole world of soap.

Whichever way we approached the notion of splitting them up, it appeared impossible to write out Ernie without losing Emily. Eileen Derbyshire, of course, wanted to stay, and it seemed very unfair even to contemplate losing her because of Stephen's principles. Life would have been made a great deal easier for everyone if they simply stayed together. The problem seemed insoluble, and occupied everyone's mind for weeks.

What were the alternatives to splitting up this clearly till-death-us-do-part pair?

Perhaps Ernie could emigrate; perhaps he could take a job abroad, or even elsewhere in the country. Wherever he might be sent, it seemed inconceivable that Emily wouldn't go too, or at least be expected to join him in the not too distant future.

Finally it was John Stevenson, one of our regular writers, who tackled the thorny problem and telephoned me to say: 'There's only one way out of this and Ernie has to die.'

I had to admit I had been thinking the same dark thoughts, but when John arrived at the studios an hour later poor old Ernie was as good as in his grave. It was simply a matter of how he should die. John outlined a very dramatic story, in which Ernie would be fatally wounded by two young armed raiders who would panic during an attempted wages snatch at Mike Baldwin's factory.

It all sounded extremely neat, but on reflection it left me with almost as big a dilemma as the one it was intended to solve. Violence on that scale had never had a place in Coronation Street and my first reactions were against a shooting of any kind. A subtle and very persuasive argument changed my mind.

There was to be none of the usual television drama of cops and robbers; no car chases leaving skid marks all over Weatherfield. It was decided that in the aftermath of the shooting we would stay in the Street reflecting on the utter futility of Ernie's death and concentrate on portraying the desolation and immense sadness it had caused.

It only remained for me to choose the moment to tell Stephen his character had to die. He happened to be taking a two-week break at his home in Stratford-on-Avon, and I decided it would be unforgivable to break the news over the 'phone, or even in a letter. I opted to wait until his return. It was a mistake, and a very painful one for all concerned.

My timing had failed to take into account the activities of the Granada mole who had been burrowing away once more and, no doubt for a fat fee, tipped off the press. A reporter from a national newspaper tracked me down to the upstairs room of a pub near the studios which the writers and I often used as a bolt-hole for planning meetings; safe, we thought, from telephones, or newspapermen.

Suddenly the door opened and there stood the newsman, a photographer at his side. They explained that they already had a confirmed story that Ernie was about to die. Coronation Street always employed a policy of never giving away advance story-lines under any circumstances, and although their facts were essentially correct I was not prepared to confirm or deny their speculation, let alone elaborate on the story they had. I never thought for one moment that they would find Stephen's home telephone number and bluntly ask the actor how he felt about Ernie being killed off.

Stephen was understandably shocked. When he telephoned the studios for confirmation, the office tracked me down, and explained that he was very angrily waiting for an explanation from me. I could only apologise for the awful manner in which he had heard.

Being sorry fell far short of repairing the damage. Stephen thought we were calling his bluff in the most Machiavellian way and the suspicions hurt him deeply. Although he had chosen to be written out in defence of his principles, I don't think he imagined his character would be called upon to give his life for them. I suspected Stephen secretly hoped the contract system might one day fall into line and give him the opportunity to return.

I asked him to come to Manchester that afternoon, and booked him into the Midland. Face to face, I could explain why there was no alternative to Ernie's death. We talked over every possible scenario, and in the end he reluctantly agreed that, to save Emily, we really had to kill Ernie off.

Nothing, however, in our past experience prepared us for the audience's reaction. This was the first violent death of a major, well-loved Coronation Street character. It was as if half the families in Britain had been suddenly bereaved.

One lady from Yorkshire who succeeded in getting a call answered by our beleaguered switchboard broke down in tears. She cried bitterly a second time while watching a recording of her beloved Ernie's death, but this time her sorrow was captured on film. Norman Swallow was as amazed as anyone at the depth of feeling the murder had aroused when he began his documentary.

When her tears had dried and outrage took over, the Yorkshire housewife vowed, 'If I ever get my hands on that Bill Podmore I'll . . .'

A few days later her wish was granted. As part of a fascinating insight into how the death of a fictional character could touch so many hearts, Norman brought her and other mourners to the set to complete his programme.

There, sadness turned to laughter. A knock at the door of number three was answered, of course, by a smiling Ernest Bishop, alive and well. They chatted like old friends on the doorstep, and a few moments later the woman who had wanted my blood met me by chance in the studio foyer and said, 'It's all right, love, I've forgiven you. I've just seen Ernie and everything's fine.'

In the end even Stephen Hancock seemed to enjoy his own passing. He turned up at Ernie's funeral and watched fascinated from the cover of some trees as the coffin was lowered.

As 'Godfather' and producer, Bill Podmore accepts the Pye Award, won by Coronation Street in 1979

8

THE GODFATHER

The nickname of 'Godfather' was coined by the press, and so neatly fitted the headlines that it was consigned to the glossary of pseudonyms to be used whenever my name was mentioned. But the image of a benevolent, or even malevolent, autocrat ruling a tiny cobblestone kingdom in the make-believe world of Weatherfield probably raised more laughs than it ever caused harm.

All powerful I certainly was. For thirteen years I had the final word in Coronation Street, and providing it was within the fairly wide-ranging boundaries of Granada's company policy, I was free to make virtually any decision I thought necessary.

But that is a producer's job. It was up to me to organise every aspect of the show, to hire artists, find writers, engage directors. When things went wrong, that was my responsibility too. The buck stopped at my desk.

The driving force was the programme itself. Had it ever been allowed to stand still, that would have meant curtains for everyone. One of the secrets of its incredible history hinges on never ignoring the need for change. Coronation Street is based on the often tough life in a working-class terrace and, as in its real-life models, there are births, marriages and deaths. Sometimes people leave home, and occasionally whole families move in and out. But when such moves happen in Coronation Street they often herald heartbreak and the dole queue for the actors and actresses involved.

There will always be someone ready to claim that I occasionally abused my power, and perhaps I did. But although I may have made a few mistakes with the hirings, I don't think I was ever particularly ruthless with the sackings.

I have always thought the firings the hardest and often saddest part of a producer's job. Rarely did anyone deserve it, and it was the one aspect of the job which never rested easily in my hands.

Perhaps Stephen Hancock had his sweet revenge for his character's demise, since Ernie's killing earned me my sinister nickname.

The death was certainly out of place in the cosy atmosphere of Coronation Street, and many thought me a cold-blooded thug to have sanctioned his shooting.

From then on, the public saw me (via the press) as a ruthless mafia-type, waiting to pounce on any actor or actress who dared step out of line. The truth was dramatically different and thankfully the cast have always treated the name as a joke.

Kissing, however, suddenly took on a new meaning. Actors and actresses are naturally affectionate people, who think nothing of greeting even distant acquaintances with a kiss on the cheek. Within the mafia, a peck on both cheeks meant the kiss of death, and for a long time I rarely got nearer the cast than a handshake without some crack being made about the Godfather. It became a running joke.

They also, superstitious lot, decided it must be bad luck to move house to Chinley. I had made my home in the peaceful Derbyshire village; the perfect escape from the pressures of the Street. It became just a little embarrassing when Cheryl Murray, who played Elsie Tanner's flighty young lodger, Suzie Birchall, decided to follow suit. She bought a new house just up the road and as I watched her move in I wondered how on earth I could break the news that her Coronation Street career was all but over.

There was a general feeling amongst the team that the Suzie Birchall character had run out of steam. Every possible story-line had been exploited, and with fresh plans to change the Tanner household, Suzie had to go. It merely remained for me to tell the actress the news.

A year or so earlier, the subject of contracts had come up in conversation as Cheryl and I strolled to one of the cast's favourite watering holes at the Film Exchange. Cheryl said she was debating whether to stay and risk being type-cast as Suzie, or make a clean break to find work in less prominent areas of television.

The prospect of leaving the security of the Street was obviously not causing her sleepless nights then, so why should she be bothered now? I comforted myself with that, though I feared I might be wrong.

I was indeed. Cheryl was devastated. Many months earlier she had made her own decision to stay, and I think that possibly lulled her into a false sense of security that she could perhaps play Suzie for as long as she liked.

The tears came in the privacy of my office. It was hard enough telling my new neighbour that our paths would have to separate; it wasn't made any easier when she sobbed out the added worry that only the day before she had signed a mortgage loan which matched her Coronation Street salary.

I felt as terrible as she did. I imagine she confided her troubles hoping to change my mind, but there was no possibility of that. The end of Suzie Birchall had been plotted long before she signed with the building society, and although it was damned hard luck the decision was final. In total innocence 'the Godfather' had struck again.

It was a far cry from one of my earliest 'contract killings'. As I have said, I brought Madge Hindle into the Street. The writers tired of her marriage to Councillor Roberts when it didn't prove, storywise, as fertile a ground as we had hoped, and we decided to make Alf either a widower or a bachelor again.

I knew Madge well, and came straight to the point: 'How do you fancy being killed off?'

She didn't. But there were no tears; she took it straight on the chin. If only it were always so.

If time proved anything, I think it underlined that the decisions to kill off characters were correct. Alf Roberts emerged into the sunlight from the shadows of a rather humdrum marriage, and eventually with his brash new bride, Audrey, became the wonderful cornerstone character he is today.

Time, however, will never rub out the casting mistakes we made. I hope and think they were rare. But when I decided to bring back Wendy Jane Walker to play Susan, Ken Barlow's grown-up daugh-

Susan and Mike Baldwin: the Street's mismatch

ter, everyone, including me, soon realised I had dropped an almighty clanger. Originally she had played a youngster, and briefly re-emerged at the wedding of Ken and Deirdre. But when the writers suggested we resurrect the ever-simmering feud between Ken and Mike Baldwin, we chose the wrong person to set the old enemies at each other's throats.

Wendy Jane looked sugar and spice and all things nice. It wasn't her fault she was young and relatively inexperienced. Having played the young Susan at her father's wedding, she was re-engaged for continuity reasons to play the part again years later. Unfortunately the scenarios she was expected to act out were far too dramatic, and it was asking too much.

For Mike to have taken a serious interest in this young lady in the first place was stretching credibility. Had she been a vamp, a dark-haired Lolita with a heaving bosom, the age gap might have been ignored. But as the story unfolded they became more and more obvious as Coronation Street's least compatible couple.

On the plus side, it allowed us to build some excitingly dramatic tension between Barlow and Baldwin, but eventually everyone realised that the marriage could never work. Johnny Briggs was very patient. He had recognised it was wrong from the start, and I eventually had to agree with him. But wherever he could he gave Wendy Jane a shoulder to lean on, and put a great deal of effort into helping her through the more difficult scenes.

The decision to break up the marriage was made at a long-term story conference. Sitting around a table it is so easy coldly and clinically to map out the lives, and even deaths, of fictitious folk. But the hard ball always bounces back into the producer's court when the drama becomes painfully real and the artist has to be warned that the future of their character is no longer solely in their hands.

It may sound cruel but, for security reasons, the long-term strategy for any character – star or bit-part player – is rarely revealed before the scripts have finally been commissioned.

I knew Wendy Jane was going to be hurt and upset.

Contracts for Coronation Street staff are normally signed in November, which means it is usually July, or August at the latest, when we consider the vexed question of who goes and who stays.

Noticeably, about this time, some of the less entrenched stars begin to look a little nervously over their shoulders. A message to the green room inviting an individual to pop up and meet Bill Podmore for a chat is suspected as meaning that 'the Godfather' is about to strike again, and received, if half-jokingly, with the gloom and doom of a black-bordered envelope.

I'm sure Wendy Jane Walker must have had some fears for her future, but my careful plans to make the blow as gentle as possible went to waste. To say she was stunned is an understatement.

Wendy Jane may have looked something of a lame duck on screen, but she had settled into the cast, and though she may have had misgivings about the security of her character, she was thoroughly enjoying fame, fortune and showbiz glamour.

The tears came first and then she actually began to shake. It was so upsetting to watch someone break down so completely that I seriously thought of packing the whole thing in myself. I had experienced some bad moments breaking this kind of news, but nothing like this. At least thirty minutes passed before Wendy could bring her emotions under control and brave facing the cast. They must have sensed what was coming. Back in the green room the welcome was Kleenex and sympathy.

Her exit story didn't make Wendy Jane's life any easier. She was to bow out with a very strong and controversial story involving abortion. There were some heavily emotional scenes and for a young, inexperienced actress they must have been an immense strain.

Added to this, Wendy Jane must have had the overwhelming feeling that every line took her a step closer to the hangman's noose. The combination made her final scenes less than convincing, and I suspect in the end it was something of a relief for her to say goodbye again to Susan Barlow.

Saying farewell was never easy, and on many occasions I was the one left sad and disappointed. In fact the number of actors and actresses who made their own unexpected exits far outnumbered those who perhaps left my office feeling angry and betrayed.

I often wonder if, had I listened to Geoffrey Hughes's misgivings about Eddie Yeats's marriage to Marion, he might still be starring in Coronation Street. An even greater imponderable is whether Hilda Ogden would have stayed too.

Stan and Hilda were one of the great comedy couples. In my book they rivalled Morecambe and Wise. But Bernard Youens's health had been failing for

Eddie, Hilda and Stan; had Eddie stayed single, might Hilda be with us yet?

some time, threatening the possibility that illness might split them up. My long-term plan was for Eddie Yeats to take over as comic-relief lodger. It just might have worked, and Jean Alexander's wonderful character might still have been bottoming out the Rovers and mopping up every morsel of Coronation Street's gossip.

I'm afraid Eddie's wedding put paid to that. Geoffrey was never happy with the marriage. He saw Eddie as a bachelor, and in the end decided to head off for pastures new. It was a great blow to the programme, but there are few blandishments to offer an artist who has made up his or her mind to leave.

Many do fear type-casting, but in Geoffrey's case his commitment to the Manchester studios kept him too long apart from his family and farm in Northamptonshire. Geoffrey was such a wonderful character-actor he would never have had any problem finding work, but many have found themselves in the wilderness after waving farewell to the Street. Giving up the security of the Street is a brave thing to do. In a profession where nine out of ten are on the dole it's almost impossible for a jobbing actor to go out into the theatre or other areas of television and pick up a salary to match the one he's left behind.

Peter Armitage was an actor who left a particularly bitter taste in my mouth. He was the nearest we ever reached to replacing Len Fairclough and I had worked on the basis that Peter would be staying for a long time.

He had promised me as much when we first talked about him taking on the part of Bill Webster. He had just returned from many months wandering through Australia and when I offered him the job I made it plain that I wasn't prepared to build a completely new family around him unless he could give me a long-term commitment. As far as I was concerned that meant at least six or seven years, and Peter was only too happy to say, 'Absolutely fine. That's just what I need.'

We set it all up, and just when everything was going he announced he'd had enough. Quite honestly I don't think anyone could pin Peter down for any length of time. He has a built-in wanderlust. But I paid dearly for my mistake.

He was very apologetic; but not only was he writing himself out, his family had to go too. I could not afford to keep them without a strong father-figure and eventually Kevin, played by Michael le Vell, was the only one we could save.

9

TRIANGLES

If there was a spare bedroom at number one Coronation Street, I'm sure Ken Barlow would have installed a personal bodyguard long ago.

Ken was the young firebrand who came for just a few weeks and went on to make a career out of overstaying his welcome. He is the last of the original cast to remain with the serial, and must rate as one of soap opera's greatest survivors. In the whole history of Coronation Street – and at the time of writing that spans a remarkable twenty-nine years – Ken has side-stepped more assassination attempts than JR Ewing, and I'm sure that clandestine plans for half those little coups never even reached his ears.

Bill Roache originally played the local lad with the right balance of brains and push to have won a place at university. Educationally he was a cut above the rest of the Street, and when the original programme makers realised what a wonderfully contrasting character he would make, it was decided he should stay. Ken finally came home with a second-class honours degree in English and history, and from that moment the question of what Ken did next became a nagging headache for what turned out to be a long line of writers and producers.

In the earliest days he represented youth's left-wing voice of protest – Ban the Bomb and anti-Vietnam war demon-

strations. But when all that became old hat, Ken was cloaked in the respectability of a schoolteacher until just about every credible story-line and passing love affair had been thoroughly played out.

Bill has described his character as a one-man Greek tragedy, and that's hardly surprising when so many of those close to him have died. Ken's mum, Ida, fell under the wheels of a bus; his father, Frank, died after winning the premium

The young Ken Barlow

bonds; his first wife, Valerie, was electro-cuted, and his second, Janet, eventually committed suicide some years after their divorce. Even his younger brother, David, popped his clogs in a car crash.

Ken can count himself very lucky that his name hasn't appeared in the obitu-ary columns too.

Even during his days as a school-teacher, the question had to be asked whether someone like Ken would ever have made his home in a place like Coronation Street. Surely he would have aspired to a modest semi in suburbia? It never seemed quite credible that he would have settled for a two-up, two-down terrace. This incongruity is even more pronounced now he's a successful newspaper proprietor.

Over the years there have been various debates as to whether Ken should be killed off, but he lives a charmed life, and someone has always come up with an idea to save him.

There was even a time when Grana-da's top brass made some playful remarks that he should be chopped. It is normally the tabloid press who take a day-to-day interest in the affairs of Coro-nation Street. When *The Times* itself thun-dered that Ken was very boring, word filtered down from the sixth floor that they would sanction any murderous plot I cared to dream up.

I concluded that they were joking, and in any case I thought that losing Ken Barlow wasn't the answer. However, I did have a long chat with Bill Roache about what he could do to help himself. It is up to the writers to give life and sparkle to a character, and I was well aware of their constant battle to keep the character of Ken alive and kicking. But the way the actor presents those ideas on screen is just as important. Ken didn't seem to be showing any affection for Deirdre, and it was no fault of the production team that there seemed to be no warmth in their marriage. That was up to the actor.

Ken rarely so much as put an arm around his wife; and apart from that, he always appeared far too formally dres-sed for someone supposedly relaxing at home after a day's work. No one was more surprised than Bill when he real-ised his character had become so wooden; he simply hadn't noticed. From there on he wore pullovers instead of a jacket, and began to show a great deal more affection for his family. These little changes helped enormously but they could not solve the underlying problem; Ken Barlow had become very boring indeed.

It was Bill Roache's patience which finally snapped. He came to me com-plaining bitterly that Ken was all but dead on his feet, and pleaded for a story-line which would snatch him from the shadows and put some excitement back into his life. I decided to make him more boring than ever.

I called the writers together, and we sweated over how Ken could be rescued. Finally we decided his wife should have an affair. All we had to do was strip Ken of what little get up and go he had left, then point Deirdre in the direction of that ageing Romeo, Mike Baldwin.

Bill Roache was horrified; I could but appeal for his trust and pray I was right. I knew that once we had dragged Ken Barlow down to rock bottom there was only one way he could go, and that was up. He would throw himself tooth and nail into a battle to save his marriage and, when it was over, re-emerge as one of the strongest characters in the pro-gramme.

I don't think Bill was convinced until we began to see how our audience was reacting. From the outset, everyone but Bill agreed an affair was a provocative and potentially explosive idea. But no one imagined just how sensational it would turn out to be. The great love triangle gripped the nation like no other story had ever done, and even Bill found himself completely caught up in the emotion of it all. In fact I knew he was thoroughly enjoying himself.

I had expected angry protests from the Church and mail by the sackload from viewers complaining that an affair and the prospect of a family being broken up were not suitable for Coronation Street. Exactly the opposite happened. The nation sat back fascinated. Every agony aunt and television pundit was caught up in the breathtaking will-she-won't-she of Deirdre's dilemma. I expected everyone to advise her to cut and run for the shelter of Ken's arms. They might be boring but at least they were safe. I was quite wrong.

Britain had its moral temperature taken, and unashamedly bubbled over with enthusiasm for a spot of naughties. One newspaper conducted a survey amongst its readers and concluded over-whelmingly that Deirdre shouldn't give a second thought to ditching her boring old hubby and running off with her lover while she had the chance.

The ratings went through the roof and the press loved it. Marriage guidance counsellors were called in for their opin-ions, leading psychiatrists consulted. A London bishop appealed for things not to get too far out of hand, and one of the Street's most eminent fans, the late Poet Laureate, Sir John Betjeman, pinned his flag firmly to Ken's mast: 'He's a nice man, and deserves better.'

When speculation had reached its height, even *The Times* felt obliged to give its readers a blow-by-blow, kiss-by-kiss rundown on the situation. No question since 'Who shot JR?' had aroused so much speculation. One national Sunday newspaper which had for years pub-lished our plots in advance, had the tongue-in-cheek temerity to tell its read-ers that for once it wasn't going to reveal the ending. The editor had enough sense to realise that the whole of Britain was thoroughly enjoying hanging on to the edge of its seats wondering if dreary Deirdre would find true love at last. Such was the cliffhanger that when Ken finally won the day a message was flashed up a mile away on the giant scoreboard at Manchester United's Old Trafford ground. 'Ken and Deirdre – REUNITED.' The fans roared their approval.

With all the hullabaloo going on around me, my real fascination concen-trated on the characters themselves.

In the pressure-cooker atmosphere of a long-running soap it is hardly surpris-ing if some of the actors and actresses become so wrapped up in their charac-ters that at times it is difficult even for them to judge where the illusion begins and ends. In any other area of the theatre or television drama artists can immerse themselves in a character but re-emerge days, or perhaps weeks, later to clothe themselves in a new, often totally different identity. But in soap series the cast are expected to live for years with the same shadow. They become fiercely defensive towards their characters and very often during emotion-al scenes you begin to wonder whether the character has taken over completely.

Bill Roache has lived with Ken Barlow for almost half his lifetime. It is hardly surprising that more than a veneer of each character has rubbed off on the other. He became so wrapped up in the fight to save his marriage, I'm sure there

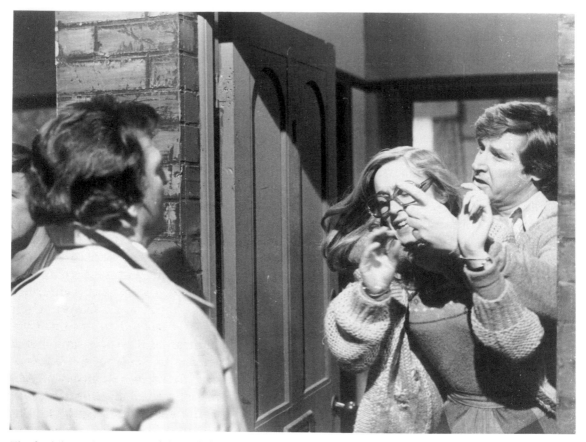

The final dramatic moments of the Mike/Deirdre/Ken triangle

were moments when it became almost completely real to him.

Mike Baldwin has been Ken's arch-enemy so long that it clearly spills over into the actors' lives. Johnny Briggs and Bill Roache are totally different characters, and not that far removed from the roles they play. They have fallen out so many times on screen that even in the green room there is little love lost between them. Self-discipline has never allowed the situation to bubble into anything more serious than the odd cross word, but even a casual observer is unlikely to miss the state of armed neutrality between them.

When emotions run high it touches everyone. At the height of the story, old Albert Tatlock was so touchingly con-fused by everything going on around him, he gave Ken and Deirdre a piece of his mind to help him reach some under-standing of why the two people he loved most seemed hell-bent on wrecking their lives. Mervyn Watson, who took over the production chair when I retired, was standing next to me at rehearsals. The scene was deeply moving even in the stark atmosphere of the rehearsal room. As it ended we caught each other, rather embarrassingly, with tears in our eyes. But when emotions become so charged they bounce off the walls, it's impossible not to be swept along.

Soap actors and actresses do undoubtedly lose themselves within their characters, and raw emotion can push them over that ill-defined frontier of reality. Usually they are the first to recognise when they have crossed the dividing line. They may later step back, physically and emotionally drained, just as Anne Kirkbride did recently when Deirdre was trapped and in danger from a man she had tried to help in her work as a councillor. But given a few minutes' breathing space or a good night's sleep, readjusting to their real selves is not usually a problem.

On one occasion it went much further, and my plans to marry Len Fairclough to Rita sparked one of the most perplexing incidents in my years with Coronation Street. I still find it difficult to come up with a satisfactory explanation.

There was unexpected resistance to the wedding plans from the start. Peter Adamson and Barbara Knox were horrified at the thought, and a great deal of gentle persuasion was needed to lead them up the aisle. The strangest opposition came from a totally unexpected source.

Pat Phoenix was furious. She hated the idea, and allowed herself to become irrationally jealous. If there is any sensible conclusion to be drawn, then it is a disturbing one. It was almost as if Elsie Tanner had taken over the reins, and Pat was powerless to stop it.

Peter and Barbara argued that a wedding could be the beginning of the end for their characters. Len and Rita were cornerstones of the Street, and they imagined that a marriage could chip the bedrock away. Their individual independence within the programme would disappear first and that, they feared, would be swiftly followed by a watering down of their story-lines. Frankly, they didn't want to share.

I explained at length that this was far from the case and that both would retain their separate areas of operation – Rita in the Kabin with Mavis, Len in his builder's yard. The dramatic change of role would give them extra story-lines constructed around their marriage and home life. I knew every fan would be enthralled, and I wasn't wrong.

Oddly enough, it was a prospect Pat couldn't handle at all.

Len and Elsie had almost married each other a couple of times during their long and close relationship and, for twenty years or more, there had always been a vague will-they-won't-they-marry situation. During her glorious reign as the Street's good-time girl with a heart of gold, Elsie tangled with at least twenty boyfriends and lovers. But when the affairs crashed it was always Len's shoulder she borrowed to cry on. Even when Elsie married, Len was hovering in the background as soul-mate, waiting to pick up the pieces. Now, however, Len was going to the altar. Elsie's anger would have been understandable. But for it to come from the actress who played her was astonishing.

Pat saw the presence of a single Len Fairclough as an integral part of her own character's image. Though they had never married Pat always saw the situation as Len and Elsie, a couple never to be split, and reacted as if part of her own life was being cut away. It seemed that she simply couldn't be rational about the matter. It was more than she could handle emotionally, and the day the wedding was shot, she sent a message to the studio and the church where it was being filmed, to say she was ill.

I couldn't believe it then, and I still don't. Pat was such a trouper she would have crawled to the studios on her hands and knees over broken glass rather than admit any illness had beaten her. Sickness was not a word in her vocabulary. She suffered constantly from a back

Another heartbreak for Elsie – and Len picks up the pieces

injury, but even when she was in agony she simply swallowed pain killers like Smarties and carried on.

Just for the moment, there wasn't time to reason why or what sickness had struck Pat Phoenix down. All I could do was press the panic button. Pat had important lines to say, and the script had to be rewritten as the guests were assembling in church.

A wedding without Elsie was unthinkable, but the unthinkable had happened and it wasn't until much later that I gave myself the chance to mull over the emotional trauma Pat must have gone through. To be jealous of the marriage must have been puzzling enough for her, but to be unable to face the ceremony must have been crushing. No one will ever convince me that Pat was ill that day, unless the trauma could be expressed as an illness in itself. I felt it was so sensitive, even years later I never dared embarrass her by asking what really went through her mind.

The missing Elsie even caused a

headache for the *TV Times*. In those days, arranging and printing colour pictures was more complicated than it is today, and this was one wedding the magazine could not afford to miss. To help meet the deadlines I set up the wedding photographs in full costume well ahead of the filming.

Pat's emotions had not yet taken over, and there she was, standing prominently centre right of the bride and groom.

If twenty million viewers were not going to see Elsie at the wedding, *TV Times* readers were not going to have the pleasure either. In a very clever bit of cutting, Elsie was given the chop. If anyone still has the picture, minute traces of the operation can be found on the pavement. A couple of paving stones are distinctly narrower than the rest.

Off Down Under – Harold and Mary Wilson with Jim Callaghan on the steps of No. 10 bid farewell to Doris Speed, Arthur Leslie, Harry Kershaw and Pat Phoenix

10

BROADENING THE MIND –
IN SINGAPORE

I joined Coronation Street with no more ambitious travel plans than perhaps the occasional summer break to the beaches of Spain. Weatherfield is anything but exotic; its residents dream of Blackpool not Bali.

But the programme had acquired a global following, and no matter how far afield it was broadcast, I seemed destined to follow. I never dreamed that I might get to the other side of the world; Coronation Street was to sweep me four times around the globe.

I was not on the first tour, in 1965, which took place at the invitation of Australian television with all the trappings of a state visit. The party of Pat Phoenix, Doris Speed and Arthur Leslie together with producer Harry V. Kershaw, were given a send-off do by Harold Wilson and Jim Callaghan at 10 Downing Street, a second by the Australian High Commissioner, and fêted throughout Australia.

The second trip, in 1980, was more of a roller-coaster ride. *TV Times* had decided to celebrate the two-thousandth episode by taking a handful of faces from Britain's most famous Street and photographing them in the palm-fringed, five-star luxury of Singapore.

Pat Phoenix, Anne Kirkbride, Johnny Briggs and I set off in a state of high excitement. One slight hitch was our discovery that the five-star aspect didn't quite start at Heathrow. We had been booked tourist class, which didn't go down too well with the stars. But for ten days we enjoyed a heady mixture of sunshine and high living in one of the most exotic cities on earth.

I don't think a Coronation Street star could safely walk unrecognised anywhere on this planet, Singapore not excepted. The island is just one of the unlikely places where the programme has been transmitted. Somehow, though, they managed to dub it with the wrong language and the majority of folk in the Coronation Streets of the city couldn't understand a word. The subtitles were in Mandarin, one of the city's four official languages, in Chinese characters down the left-hand side of the screen.

It left no room for subtitles in the native Tamil. The demand was so great from the Tamil speakers that a solution had to be found. Local radio came up with an ingenious answer. As the television pictures were transmitted, it broadcast a simultaneous soundtrack read live by a translator. Most folk watched with the television turned down and the radio on. Which goes to show the remarkable lengths to which some people will go to follow the lives of ordinary folk on the other side of the world.

On this trip we were far from ordinary,

Annie, Jack and Ena subtitled in Mandarin

as our hotel, the Hyatt Regency, was keen to emphasise. The rooms were splendid, and in pride of place on the writing tables were leather-bound writing cases. I opened mine to find 'Bill Podmore' embossed in gold on the notepaper; and just in case anyone missed that, it was in gold on the envelope too.

It was rather splendid, if a little over the top, but when we assembled in the bar later the four of us chorused: 'Have you seen the notepaper?'

Pat was so impressed she ordered more. Anne was slightly less enthusiastic. 'They've spelt my name the Chinese way,' she complained as we roared with laughter. 'Kirkblide . . . They managed

one R, but they obviously couldn't cope with two.'

That wasn't Anne's only problem with the language barrier. As we were the guests of *TV Times*, that is the name Anne signed when she ordered from room service. The hotel accounts department rang her room wondering why they could find no record of a Miss T.V. Times in the register.

Despite the heat and humidity which can be very oppressive we did the full tourist trip. We sailed sampans to the islands, rode the mountain cable car, and in the Tiger Balm gardens, the city's answer to Disneyland, we rechristened the enormously fat Buddha, Stan Ogden.

Singapore was the first Far Eastern trip any of us had taken and the sights and sounds were intoxicating. In those days one of the great down-town attractions was Boogy Street, an area famous for its transvestites.

For reasons I have never been able to fathom, the editor of *TV Times* ordered his cameraman not to return without a picture of Johnny Briggs with one of the Boogy Street beauties. Johnny was as perplexed as anyone but agreed to go along with the bizarre idea.

The creatures of Boogy Street begin their parade on the stroke of midnight, very exotic and a great crowd-puller. They looked like the most beautiful girls imaginable, but of course they are not. Pat and Anne were as keen as any to watch this spectacle, and we sat at a pavement café, next to the crew of a British tanker, who instantly recognised us.

We explained our plan. The first mate whispered to me, sounding concerned: 'Now you know these girls are really fellas, don't you?' I replied that I did, to which he rather sheepishly admitted, 'I wish someone had told *me* the first time I came down here.'

The time came to organise our little modelling session and I went over to a statuesque 'lady', followed by Johnny and Paul Stokes, the *TV Times* photographer, hung about with three Nikons and a flash gun.

'Excuse me, but can I have a photograph of you with my friend?' I enquired of the transvestite.

'Yes you can,' he agreed. 'But him professional photographer and it's thirty dollars.'

Pat Phoenix, Johnny Briggs, Anne Kirkbride and Bill Podmore relax in Singapore (Photo: Bill Podmore)

The going rate was apparently ten, and I tried the tack that Paul was simply an over-enthusiastic amateur.

Finally the transvestite made a lunge for me shouting, 'You cheeky chappy.' He grabbed me in a private place, which took me by surprise as you can imagine. But having had a few drinks I decided to join in the game and grabbed him in the same area – only to discover he'd had a drastic operation. My look of horror was the only evidence Pat and Anne needed. They shrieked with laughter.

I was so shocked, I didn't realise this was a well-rehearsed routine, and in seconds an accomplice had swooped from behind and picked my pockets clean. We never did get the picture.

The journey home was a nightmare. Johnny had left a day earlier with the photographer, and I thought I had been fortunate, squeezing in an extra day. How wrong I was. The extra hours in Singapore were fine. At the airport, Murphy's Law took over; if anything could go wrong, it most certainly did.

I have heard all sorts of reasons for flight delays, but the story of the jumbo which took off carrying a little too much weight was almost entertaining in its freshness. Apparently the flight engineer had miscalculated his take-off weight and at the critical moment gravity overcame the physics of flight. The aircraft had just managed to leave the runway when it flopped back down, leaving a huge dent in the runway. Luckily no one was hurt, but the whole airport was thrown well behind schedule while they hauled away the mangled plane, then filled the holes in the concrete.

Finally, tempers frayed from boredom and heat, we boarded, relieved to be starting the long haul home. Murphy had other ideas.

The tourist cabin was packed, mainly with Sikhs returning to India for a religious festival, and our seats were in the very last row, next door to the toilets. Pat was furious and I have to admit none of us was very happy. That was only the start of our troubles.

We sat there for the whole night complaining to each other that this was no way to treat the stars of Britain's favourite soap opera. First, an engine refused to start. Rather than unload the passengers while it was fixed, the cabin crew served a very late dinner. Then the flight crew, who had waited patiently with us, didn't have enough time left in the strict flying schedules to take the plane to its first stop at Bombay. We waited while a new crew were rustled up.

To cap it all, there was a complete nutcase sitting in the next seat, a British engineer; rude, overbearing, loud and aggressive. He behaved appallingly. It appeared he had been mixing drinks with some medicine he needed to take, and when we finally got into the air at eight in the morning, he collapsed unconscious.

A doctor pronounced him to be in no great danger, and he was unceremoniously stuffed behind our seats to sleep it off. To meet with safety regulations he was hauled back to his seat at Bombay, and I had to truss him up with a blanket to prevent him slumping over the lady next to him.

When we touched down at Dubai he woke up shouting, 'Who did this to me?' The cabin crew had had enough and he would probably have ended up in a Dubai prison had an Australian nurse, who had been on the plane for two days, not offered to take care of him until the effect of the drink and pills had worn off.

That happened on the homeward leg when his bleary eyes fixed on Pat. 'I know you from somewhere, don't I?' said he.

It was the only time I ever heard Pat Phoenix deny her own identity or that of Elsie Tanner. The truth only came out later when another passenger asked for her autograph.

The man was delighted to meet us, and insisted he would drive us from Heathrow to Manchester in his own car. From our seats came a chorus of: 'No thanks!'

Bill Podmore and Chris Quinten about to get very wet! (Photo: Bill Podmore)

11

CHAMPAGNE IN CANADA

A couple of years later, a Canadian company which had opened a chain of English-style pubs in Toronto asked if some of our stars could come over to lend glamour to the launch.

Julie Goodyear, then barmaid of the Rovers Return, was the obvious first choice, but as the trip sounded like fun I asked Chris Quinten and Johnny Briggs to join the party.

The Canadian Broadcasting Company has been screening the Street for many years, although at the outset their episodes lagged far behind Britain. To catch up, they screened it five times a week, and by the time we arrived the cast were almost national heroes.

Our feet didn't touch the ground from the moment we arrived. Breakfast had to be abandoned on the first morning to fit in a radio interview, and from there on we were swept along on a tidal wave of chat shows, personal appearances and autograph sessions.

The welcome was unbelievable. So many fans turned up to see us on the third floor of one department store, they bolted the doors fearing the building would collapse under the sheer weight. During 'phone-in shows the lines were jammed, and when we made personal appearances whole towns turned out to greet us.

We split up to meet all the dates, and one morning Johnny and I set off with enthusiasm to open a pub called the Manchester Arms. The owner was from Manchester, and we had a good old chin-wag about recent changes in our home city. The opening was to resemble a ship launching. Hundreds had turned out to watch the fun, and Johnny was asked if he would swing a magnum of champagne, hung on a ribbon from the eaves, at the pub wall, announcing: 'I name this pub the Manchester Arms.'

That's exactly what he did except the bottle bounced back. Everyone roared with laughter and Johnny lined up for another shot. Wallop! the bottle bounced back again; all that broke was the ribbon.

'What do you have to do to break a bottle of champagne?' Johnny pleaded to the crowd who thought the whole performance hilarious.

He picked the bottle up by the neck, walked over to the pub and was just about to smash it on a windowsill when I shouted for him to stop.

'What's the problem?' he asked.

'It'll explode. It's far too dangerous,' I warned.

I told him to stand back and throw just a little bit harder.

'Right,' he said, sufficient fury in his voice to guarantee the bottle would break, 'I name this pub – '

For the third time the bottle bounced off the brickwork as if made of rubber and landed at his feet intact.

Someone shouted,' It's a good job you can act better than you can crack champagne.'

Johnny looked beaten. He handed the bottle to me. 'Here, you have a shot.'

Johnny said his line for the fourth time, and I hurled the missile.

There was the most almighty bang and the bottle simply disappeared in the explosion. All that was left was a tiny ring of glass from the neck. The rest of the bottle, label, contents, the lot had simply disintegrated.

Johnny went white. He turned to me and said, 'Thank God you stopped me smashing it on that windowsill.'

From the first throw the contents of that bottle must have been an inferno of gas. Had it exploded in his hand I'm sure he would have been seriously injured, and possibly blinded. We made a dive for the bar.

Our thoughtful hosts had planned our trip with a rest day to break up the pace. We visited Niagara Falls – truly awesome, and quite frightening too. Julie Goodyear clung to my arm as the mist and spray swirled about us. I imagine millions of men would gladly have swapped places with me, but I can assure them that the vision of Julie in a giant sou'wester and full-length black plastic mac was so ludicrous that sex appeal went overboard.

The following day we were guests of honour at a lunch party given by the deputy premier of Ontario, Robert 'Bob' Welsh, QC, and his family at the old English town of Niagara on the Lake. They were devoted fans, and it appeared the whole town shared their enthusiasm. We were treated like royalty.

We were guests on various television chat shows, and the great surprise for

Julie Goodyear, Johnny Briggs and Chris Quinten at Niagara Falls (Photo: Bill Podmore)

me was how many questions were actually directed at me. I had fully expected to be the wallflower while Julie, Chris and Johnny stole the limelight, but the audience seemed fascinated about how the programme was put together, and I faced a barrage of questions about what had led to characters being brought in and, of course, killed off. I suspect Ernie Bishop will haunt me as long as I live; that evening I had to do some fast talking to justify why I had chosen to have him murdered.

Some years later, when I was admitted to a Manchester hospital for a minor operation, I got chatting to the man in the next bed, and discovered we lived in neighbouring villages.

'You don't happen to know a chap called Bill Podmore do you?' he enquired.

'Yes,' I replied. 'Quite well actually. As a matter of fact I am Bill Podmore.'

'Good gracious,' he said. 'So you are. Do you know, I met you in Toronto. You gave me your autograph.'

Being recognised like that was one of the pleasures of being Coronation Street's producer. My name appeared on the credits and, without wishing to appear conceited, I suppose I am now a household name; but I can choose where and when to enjoy the fame. Now and again I am recognised in the street, but for the most part I can wander freely around in anonymity. Almost all the cast are instantly recognisable, and although they enjoy the fame at first it can get very tedious.

The only actress who got away with it almost completely was Jean Alexander. She could transform herself within seconds. A touch of lipstick, a headscarf, an old mackintosh and a curler or two,

and there stood Hilda Ogden in all her pinched-mouth glory. At the end of the day the cloak of Hilda was discarded as quickly as it was created and left behind in the studio. Jean Alexander could stand on Salford station and catch her train home safe in the knowledge that none of her fellow passengers would give the elegant lady a second glance.

The rest of the cast are not so fortunate. The majority, in appearance, play little more than perhaps a slight exaggeration of their real selves, and I don't suppose dark glasses or even a false beard would be an adequate disguise.

I am in the happy position of having a name that is known to millions, and a face which is not. My appearance on Toronto television made me vulnerable for once.

Chris Quinten was enjoying himself chasing pretty girls all over Toronto one night while I joined Johnny in the hotel lounge for a nightcap. Sitting behind us was a rather severe-looking grey-haired lady, accompanied by two younger women.

She recognised me instantly. 'Mr Podmore, I just wanted to say how much I enjoyed the show this evening,' she began. 'You are obviously a very intelligent man and I think you are wonderful.'

She turned to introduce the first of her two companions and without the slightest hint of embarrassment announced: 'This is my daughter-in-law, but if you would like to take her off to bed, that's fine by me.'

I don't think I have ever been so shocked in all my life, and from the look on Johnny's face he was equally dumbfounded.

'That's a very generous gesture, madame,' I managed to say, 'but I don't think your son would be too pleased.'

Poet Laureate Sir John Betjeman, who said his idea of heaven was watching Coronation Street, meets his favourite characters, Hilda and Stan

12

FANS
IN HIGH PLACES

It was often claimed, and never denied, that when Harold Wilson was Prime Minister he conspired to bring cabinet business to a close a little before 7.30 on Monday and Wednesday evenings, and could get quite annoyed if less pressing matters of state disturbed his enjoyment of Coronation Street.

Jim Callaghan made no secret of the fact that he avidly followed the series, and when we celebrated the making of our two-thousandth episode, Margaret Thatcher sent personal congratulations from 10 Downing Street, saying, 'There must be few people in Britain who have not heard of the Rovers Return, or become involved in the lives of Ena Sharples, Albert Tatlock, Annie Walker, Elsie Tanner and Ken Barlow. To have sustained such popularity is a tremendous achievement. Long may your success continue.'

In this age of hype and superlatives, it is so easy to dismiss viewing figures, particularly when they end with a long row of noughts. They tend to roll off the tongue without thought for their true meaning.

But when you stop to think that twice every week – and now on Sunday afternoons too – almost half the people living in the British Isles stop what they are doing to sit down and follow the lives of working-class families grouped around a drab Northern backstreet, realisation begins to dawn of how much the programme has become woven into the fabric of the nation's consciousness.

Coronation Street has become a national institution, one that is fiercely defended by fans from every walk of life. It is wonderful to know that the Queen and her family, premiers, lords and earls enjoy the programme as much as its legions of devoted ordinary folk. But perhaps the most treasured compliments which have been heaped on the programme have come from the peers of the entertainment business.

The late Russell Harty once said, 'There was life before Coronation Street . . . but it didn't add up to much.' With the willing support of Michael Parkinson and Willis Hall, Russell helped found the British League for Hilda Ogden and had no trouble persuading Sir John Betjeman to become its honorary life president.

Sir John paid his own tribute to the writers and cast: 'Not a word too many. Not a gesture needless. It is the best writing and acting I could wish to see.'

More than two thousand actors and actresses have played in the series. Some very small parts have been played by very big names. Angela Douglas, wife of the late Kenneth More, played one of Dennis Tanner's girlfriends; Bill Maynard appeared as a music agent; Davy Jones of the Monkees played Ena

The cast with Sir John Betjeman (centre front) (Photo: Doug McKenzie Photographic Services Ltd)

Sharples's grandson; Prunella Scales arrived as a bus conductress; Joanna Lumley made a play for Ken Barlow, and Oscar-winning actor Ben Kingsley once chatted up Irma Barlow. The list of stars who have walked the cobbles of the Street is a long one, but sadly I never quite captured the actor who would certainly have topped our guest-of-honour list.

Annie Walker might well have taken it in her stride, and dined out on the story with the Lady Licensed Victuallers of Weatherfield for years. But the day the lovely Doris Speed came face-to-face with one of the great knights of the theatre, it left her speechless. She was sitting relaxed in the make-up department, her eyes closed, when she felt

someone touch her fingers. Almost before she could turn her head, her hand was kissed and Sir Laurence Olivier, who had crept in and taken the next chair, said graciously, 'My dear lady, I must say how much I enjoy your performance.'

He was also one of Hilda Ogden's great fans, and had Sir Laurence not been so busy drilling out the teeth of Dustin Hoffman – another one-time Street visitor – in *The Marathon Man*, he might have starred alongside Jean Alexander in an altogether sweeter role.

I first met Lord Olivier when he came to the Granada studios to film a series of classic stage plays specially adapted for television. It was while he was in make-up preparing for his role as Big Daddy in

Cat on a Hot Tin Roof that he so charmingly put a sparkle into Doris Speed's day.

I knew he was a fan, and I couldn't pass up the opportunity to ask if he would accept an invitation to appear in the show, if only for a fleeting performance. 'My dear fellow, I would love to be in it,' he announced, without a second's thought, and I immediately began the search for a suitable cameo role.

I found it while we were planning a scene where Hilda, her heart set on a colour television knocked down to £5 in Perkins' January sale, resolved to camp out overnight on the pavement. She was to be joined in her vigil, much to her annoyance, by a rather odious little tramp, and in my mind I instantly cast Sir Laurence. Heavily made up, he would never be recognised; our greatest casting coup would be revealed only when the credits rolled.

Unfortunately, his film commitments in America clashed with our dates, and the plan had to be scrapped. But before he had completed his film work for Granada I did get the chance to introduce Jean Alexander to him. Jean and I were having lunch in the Film Exchange, when she noticed Sir Laurence alone at a nearby table. Jean was genuinely thrilled just to be in the same room as the great man and told me of the time when, as a struggling and hard-up actress in London, she had queued for hours to see him in *Othello*.

For me the temptation was too much. I took her arm and said, 'Come on, I'll introduce you.'

Jean was almost overcome with embarrassment. 'Oh, don't be silly, Bill, I daren't,' she scolded.

I persisted and was delighted I did. I've never seen Jean so thrilled. I took her over to Sir Laurence and said, 'Hello, I'd like to introduce you to Jean Alexander.'

He rose smiling, took her hand and said, 'We won't need any introductions. Wonderful lady, please sit down.'

The street studio has always been something of a Mecca for visiting TV personalities and other VIPs. But perhaps our proudest moment was when the Queen and the Duke of Edinburgh officially opened our outdoor set in the spring of 1983.

Coronation Street, complete with the frontages of the Rovers Return and Alf Roberts's corner shop, had been rebuilt down to the last little detail from 50,000 second-hand Salford bricks and 6,500 slates reclaimed from demolition areas around the real Archie Street – the backstreet little more than a mile away on which the show was originally based.

The royal party was coming to Manchester to open a new library at the university, but part of the day was set aside for the Queen and Duke to tour the Castlefield area, just along the road from Granada, where the remains of a Roman fort were being restored, and the neighbouring City Hall and surrounding railway properties had been refurbished as museums of aerospace and industry.

The Lord Lieutenant of Lancashire was checking over the route for the walkabout when he realised the new Coronation Street set adjoined the railway yard and the site of Britain's first passenger railway station. He suspected the Queen would be delighted to see the home of Britain's favourite programme and arrangements were put in hand.

It seemed impossible that the Queen herself would want to walk down our humble Street, but in anticipation it was decorated with flower baskets and flags, while everyone from the show waited in

The Queen and Duke of Edinburgh take a stroll down the cobblestones

high excitement. She arrived smiling and elegant, examining the whole place with obvious fascination. We had heard she enjoyed the programme, but when I later had the opportunity, I didn't think it protocol to ask.

The cast lined up along the pavement nervously waiting to be introduced. I held my breath. The cobblestones of Coronation Street are not the easiest things to walk on, and the Queen wore quite high-heeled shoes. I was feeling a little quakey at the head of the line and we were all apprehensive in case she might slip.

I was to be introduced together with Harry Kershaw, Dennis Parkin, the original designer, and Tony Warren. During the first introductions, Tony was asked by Her Majesty where the real Coronation Street and Rovers Return were actually situated.

He might have said Archie Street but – he assures me, quite off the cuff – he came out with the rather eloquent reply: 'It sounds a bit crowey, Ma'am. But it's wherever you want it to be in your own heart.'

The Queen was obviously impressed, and replied with a gracious smile, 'It doesn't sound a bit crowey at all.'

I suspect the Duke must join his wife in the drawing-room of Buckingham Palace on more than a few Monday and Wednesday evenings, because he made what I considered a very perceptive comment. Instead of resorting to small talk, he raised an ever-present production problem: 'It must be very difficult to keep the programme continually fresh.'

I replied, 'Exactly. That is always our main concern and one which will never get easier as the years go by.'

The royal party walked the length of the Street, stopping to chat as the cast came forward. The weather was kind with a day of bright sunshine, but for everyone there were dark clouds on the horizon. The Falklands War was being fought in the Southern Atlantic, and some told the Queen how much they shared her concern for the safety of Prince Andrew.

Julie Goodyear was as irreverent as ever. She wore a pair of her famous earrings, with a picture of Prince Charles dangling from one ear, and Princess Di clipped to the other. It didn't go unnoti-

The Queen shakes hands with Tony Warren. With him (left to right) are Bill Podmore, Harry Kershaw and Dennis Parkin

Julie Goodyear, with her Charles and Di earrings, hopes her Majesty is amused

ced by the Queen and we half expected Bet Lynch to spend a night or two as Her Majesty's guest in the Tower of London.

As the Queen and Duke strolled down the Street, I was to follow, collecting everyone who had been spoken to and forming the cast into a group to wave goodbye. In my anxiety and enthusiasm I got a little too far ahead. I felt a firm hand on my shoulder and a plainclothes bodyguard politely but firmly said, 'I hope you don't mind but you are blocking the eye-line between myself and the Duke.'

What he meant, of course, was that at all times he wanted a clear pistol shot in case anyone made an attempt on the Duke's life. Highly unlikely along Coronation Street, but the policeman with a bulge by his breast pocket was taking no chances.

Some years earlier, when the Queen had celebrated part of her Silver Jubilee with a visit to Manchester's Palace Theatre, I had been asked if the cast would entertain her with a sketch. John Stevenson came up with a great idea based around an imaginary visit by Her Majesty to Weatherfield, and Hilda Ogden turning out at the crack of dawn to get the best vantage point to watch the parade.

There was an immediate burst of applause as the curtains opened to the haunting strains of Eric Spear's Coronation Street theme. As the sketch unfolded, every member of the case came on stage, each with a few lines of dialogue, until Eddie Yeats completed the line-up, wheeling Stan Ogden in a barrow. It brought the house down, and when I glanced over to the Royal box it was obvious that the Queen and Duke were thoroughly enjoying the entertainment.

I had been asked to select two cast members to be officially introduced backstage. I nominated Jean Alexander, the star of our part of the show, and Jack Howarth, the Street's elder statesman.

The rest were a little upset that they would not meet the Queen. I sympathised, and mentioned their disappointment to David Scase, who was producing the Palace show, and who later played our Dr Lowther. I argued that, after all, Coronation Street was probably the world's most famous television programme and I was sure the Royal couple would enjoy the opportunity to meet them all. I suggested they form a guard of honour in the foyer as the Queen and Duke left.

There were security problems which

Howard Keel leads the ladies of the cast in a knees-up

Dustin Hoffman takes a pint in the Rovers

had to be cleared with the Lord Lieutenant, but the Queen showed her appreciation by saying in a voice of mock surprise, 'Oh, I seem to have seen you all somewhere before.'

She stopped to shake hands with some of cast as she passed, and it rounded off the evening beautifully. Little did we expect we would meet her again, in Coronation Street itself.

The Rovers was usually open house to visiting stars. The splendidly lugubrious face of Alfred Hitchcock himself once peered around its doors, and a whole host of celebrities have had their photographs taken at its bar. It has never been closed to rival shows either. Howard Keel, Dallas's Clayton Farlow, has been

on the set as has Larry Hagman, the show's JR Ewing.

It was very sad that until the outdoor set was built, and taken over by Granada Tours, only visiting celebrities could visit. Members of the public simply could not be allowed on set, unless at the express invitation and under the wing of a member of the cast. So many requests came we never dared set a precedent. Many of the letters were quite heartrending. They were often made on behalf of handicapped children or disabled mums and dads. Explaining why we had to turn them all down was at times very distressing. It would have been unfair to single anyone out; the only exceptions we ever made were for people already in the studios taking part in other programmes.

13

THE DEATH
OF A GENTLEMAN

Sometimes tragedy visited the lives of the 'family' which made up our cast and production team. For me, the most heart-breaking time was when the fates so cruelly conspired against Peter Dudley.

Peter was a fine actor and a great friend. The fact that he was homosexual didn't make the slightest difference. He was held in deep and genuine affection by everyone who knew him.

Peter made no secret of his sexuality, but neither did he flaunt it. A stranger would never have guessed. When anyone who did know displayed a prejudice, he simply went to work with his sense of humour and won them over with ineffable ease. Throughout the years I knew and worked with him, I never heard a bad word spoken against him. But perhaps that made it worse, when tragedy overtook and killed this quiet, gentle man.

We first met in the late sixties when I had been invited to direct a couple of Coronation Street episodes. Peter was then an almost unknown jobbing actor working in repertory theatre.

I always regarded such a background as a plus. Coronation Street has regularly drawn from rep. All the original cast were unknowns apart from Violet Carson, but they were all experienced rep players, their faces anonymous outside the provincial theatres, and that gave the Street its essential credibility.

Had it been cast with well-known faces it would never have achieved its original impact.

Peter had an added advantage. Pat Phoenix had recognised his talent, they had become close pals, and she was carrying a torch for his career. I went to see him in theatre and wholeheartedly agreed with Pat's assessment. His acting ability was extraordinary. Pat, of course, never let me forget it. At every opportunity she would remind me that Peter was waiting in the wings, impatient for a chance to join the Street.

I bumped into him from time to time. Pat regularly threw parties at her home in Disley and Peter never passed up the chance to ask, 'You won't forget me, will you?'

At one point I did cast a small part which might have suited Peter, and not unnaturally he was bitterly disappointed. He deserved an explanation, although I don't think for one minute I convinced him that what I had in mind would be beyond his wildest dreams.

I consoled him with the promise that one day a big part would come his way. His reaction was understandable. 'Yea, yea . . . I'll believe that when it happens.' Happily it did and I've never seen a man more thrilled.

Lynne Perrie had already established the character of Ivy Tilsley, and it was decided she should come to live at

The new family at number 5: Bert, Brian and Ivy Tilsley

number five, bringing along a husband, Bert, and young son, Brian.

Peter was perfect for Bert, and swiftly proved what a terrific actor he was. He played the part with utter credibility, and with all the warmth and sympathy the scriptwriters could have hoped for. He gave us everything we wanted from the character, and the cast recognised his talent. He was the average 'little man' facing middle age with a fearful insecurity which stemmed from being made redundant from the only job he knew, a skilled operator in an engineering works.

As I have said, my office door was

always open to cast members with problems, and as time went by I became a kind of father figure to the Street 'family', used to all kinds of confessions and discussions. Even so, I was knocked sideways the morning Peter came to see me. I was reading through scripts when Carol, my secretary, popped her head round the door and said he wanted a chat. Everything seemed so normal as he came through the door, I presumed it was nothing more important than where we might go for lunch.

He had obviously managed to hold himself together until this point. But as Carol closed the door he started to crack up. He sobbed it out. 'I'm in real trouble, Bill, serious trouble.'

I thought someone close must have died. What was to come was perhaps even worse. This generous, gentle and instantly likeable man crumbled before my eyes. Things have often gone wrong for people I've been extremely fond of. Sometimes I've been able to help. But the story Peter unfolded left me feeling utterly helpless.

It was almost impossible to grasp the enormity of the mistake this man had made. Here was an actor who had achieved everything he wanted; to join Coronation Street had been his one great ambition. Peter knew he was good, knew he was right for the part and that, above all, he was a natural Coronation Street character. Now he was telling me he had jeopardised it all for what can only be described as a cheap thrill, and his whole world had come crashing down around him.

There is no polite way of explaining what Peter had done. No delicate choice of words can disguise the sordid truth. Policemen keeping watch on public toilets known to be frequented by homosexual men had accused Peter of trying to attract another man's attention by exposing himself.

It is hard for heterosexual people to understand why some homosexuals derive excitement from this, but apparently they do. I won't attempt to defend it, but Peter was charged at a time when Manchester police appeared to be conducting an all-out purge on the gay community.

The police were quite aware of the spots where these people congregated; I think it was taking surveillance too far when they climbed ladders and peered through public toilet windows. Whatever, Peter was observed in these toilets in Didsbury, a pleasant suburb south of the city centre, and charged with importuning.

He was absolutely distraught. He sat in my office head in hands, crying openly, obviously at a total loss as to how he might begin to handle the situation.

Initially I was very, very angry. My first loyalty was to Coronation Street. This was going to make headlines in the press – headlines of the worst possible kind. But there was Peter to consider. He knew he had possibly destroyed everything he had worked for.

We had a long talk. At first, he tried to convince me he had gone to the toilets innocently, in fact by accident. He stammered through a garbled and unlikely explanation; he had been travelling from Preston to his home not far from Granada's headquarters in city centre Manchester; he had arrived in Didsbury accidentally after taking a wrong exit from the motorway.

It didn't add up. I warned him not to play innocent with me of all people. If I was ever in a position where I could possibly help, I had to know the truth. I could almost have grown angry, but at that stage I don't think Peter was capable of facing the real facts.

I needed time to consider and, no less important, I needed to make those above me aware of the situation and exactly how I proposed to handle it. I had already made my decision.

The cast were beginning to talk. News, especially bad news, always travels fast. Pat Phoenix was the first to approach me. She straightforwardly asked, 'What's going to happen to him?' At that stage I could only reply that I would be seeing Peter again, and I asked him to come to my office. He was terrified and I had no wish to prolong his agony.

I said, 'Look, Peter, this time it's OK. We are going to live with it and I'll support you all the way. Your job is secure whatever happens in court. Try not to worry about it. I just want your solemn promise that something like this will never, never happen again.' He was so relieved, he broke down and cried.

Peter was fined two hundred pounds. He went to every possible length to express his gratitude to Granada and the cast for their unstinting support. He gave everyone a great big personal thank you, but that was Peter's nature and we all loved him for it.

My support for Peter was rewarded by a great many letters from viewers who did not share my tolerance. Some stated quite clearly that I must be homosexual myself, an accusation totally false. My one comfort was the realisation that I didn't share their hatred for someone different. But it seemed that very many people did harbour a prejudice, and for each person who wrote, you could be sure there were scores more fans out there thinking the same.

'How dare you support this homosexual, this filthy person who visits gents' lavatories,' came the outcry. 'Absolutely disgusting, get him off the programme,' said another. A third demanded, 'How can you have this man in a programme so well-known for its family viewing?'

To some letters I could not reply. I think I would have lost my temper. To the more reasoned I wrote back trying to explain I had simply chosen to protect someone I counted among my friends, despite his sexual leanings.

In the end my decision about Peter came down to pure professionalism. The marriage of Ivy and Bert worked remarkably well as television. Peter's handling of scenes was often brilliant. A few scenes even stand out in my mind as masterpieces. To throw all that away just because of an incident, however distasteful to the majority, did not seem fair to anyone.

Many months later, I was forced to reconsider that decision very carefully. Sadly, I had to ask myself whether I could forgive and forget for a second time. I had sincerely believed, when the court case ended, that we had heard the last of it, and was convinced Peter would never find himself in that position again. Imagine how I felt when one morning he walked into my office again.

He stood there a broken man. There isn't any other way to describe it. He broke down in a flood of tears. When I asked what was the matter his only reply was, 'I'm pleading not guilty.' I couldn't believe what I was hearing, and I didn't want to. What could I say except, 'Oh my God, you haven't done it again?'

He tried his hardest to pour out some kind of explanation, but he could hardly even speak. Eventually the appalling truth was confirmed when he said, 'I was in this place and the police were waiting for me.'

He had to rehearse and film that week, and had no alternative but to sit it out with the cast and work as best he could. Somehow he managed the scenes, but he now knew he was in very serious trouble. He protested his innocence, but had no chance of convincing anyone.

He refused to admit his guilt even privately to me. I pleaded with him, 'Peter, face the truth.' His only reply was, 'I'm finished.'

I could do nothing but wait for the court's decision. He had chosen to go to the Crown Court, rather than have magistrates deal quickly with the case. The first jury failed to agree and the judge ordered a retrial. It was never heard. The anxiety and strain had been too much for Peter, who suffered a stroke and lost the use of his left side. His recovery was only partial. His speech came back but he had almost totally lost the power of his left arm.

He believed he would make a full recovery given time and no one at the hospital was prepared to tell him anything different. His physiotherapist, a friend of mine, told me that the time allowed for a full recovery had long past. Nevertheless, Peter had to be left living in hope. If he had despaired and given up his exercises, his withered arm might have ceased to function even in a limited way.

Above all he wanted to come back to the Street, and a way had to be devised. We wrote a story-line about an air compressor exploding while Bert inflated a tyre in Brian's garage. The make-believe injury and careful camera work disguised the real reason his arm didn't work.

I was then working temporarily on a comedy series called Brass, and Mervyn Watson was caring for the day-to-day running of the Street. One morning I came in and heard from Gordon McKellar, the production manager, that Mervyn needed to see me urgently. I went straight along to his office, to be told, 'I've some sad news. Peter Dudley has died.'

The shock was devastating. I cried, and I say that without shame. It was all over. The worry of a second court case had been too much for Peter. A second stroke had stopped this sad little man's broken heart.

Peter Adamson – it was breach of contract rather than scandalous revelations unearthed by the tabloids which led to his eventual dismissal

14

A BITTER ENDING

A year before Peter Dudley's sad story, the highly publicised court appearance of another major character had caused us all much worry and distress. The bombshell which rocked the programme to its foundations dropped one Sunday morning in April 1983 when a newspaper reported that Peter Adamson had been arrested, held overnight in police cells and charged with perhaps the most distasteful offence imaginable – indecently assaulting two eight-year-old girls in a swimming pool.

The ordeal came to a close a wearisome eight months later when, wearing a top hat and an undertaker's suit, Peter tried to make light of the whole sordid affair and cheekily appeared on television to deliver his obituary for Len Fairclough on TV-am.

I listened to him, half smiling. There was no denying it contained a certain black humour which I found appealing. But the underlying bitterness, and the selfish distortion of the truth, left a very nasty taste in my mouth, and in the mouths of many of his old friends at Granada.

Peter delivered his epitaph early in December 1983, hours after Len Fairclough had been killed in a motorway crash. But what the actor failed to make clear that morning, or at any time during that traumatic year, was that if anyone was guilty of Len Fairclough's murder, it was Peter himself.

The private lives of the cast are under constant scrutiny from an eagle-eyed press, and over the years a diligent band of journalists have dug up some remarkable stories, sometimes funny, occasionally shocking. Hung in the smallest room of my home is the original of a cartoon created by the *Sun*'s Bill Caldwell. After a particularly entertaining run of what the tabloids would describe as 'shocking revelations', he had characterised the cast standing outside the Rovers waiting for their instructions before the cameras rolled. The punchline was delivered through a megaphone as the director ordered, 'Throw away your scripts. Just carry on talking about your private lives.'

Coronation Street was rarely out of the headlines, and although the cast and crew became pretty thick-skinned to whatever salacious gossip arrived next on their breakfast tables, nothing had prepared us for the news that Peter Adamson had been charged with indecent assault on children.

The Street draws together in times of trouble. Kick one, and we all limp. When the chips are down and the pressure comes from outside, the cast support each other. They know how vulnerable they all are to the attention of the press.

The allegations Peter faced transcended all that. It was a massive shock, and everyone was confused. Apart from a handful of close friends who refused to believe a word of it, no one knew whether they should openly support Peter or not. Everyone prayed the police had made some ghastly mistake, but many felt there could be no smoke without fire. Peter had never made a secret of his affection for children, and he often brought youngsters along to watch rehearsals.

The basis of the police complaint was that Peter's hands had strayed while he had been giving the girls swimming lessons. For three dreadful months he lived with the horror of this, until a Crown Court jury found him innocent. After twenty-two years playing Len Fairclough it was understandable that the majority of the public saw Len in the dock alongside Adamson. Within Granada, many felt that the good name of Coronation Street was also on trial. On the morning of the 'not guilty' verdict the news was rushed to the rehearsal room, and a great cheer went up.

A terrible cloud had been lifted, but for me the next storm was already gathering. In the weeks which followed, a series of confusing stories led the public to believe that Granada had overturned the court's acquittal and that I had sacked Peter for the disgrace he had heaped upon us.

Nothing could have been further from the truth, and although Adamson knew the exact circumstances of his departure, he never uttered a word which might have led his fans to the truth. His obituary poem clearly stated that he felt we had thrown him to the wolves.

In fact, his future with the programme had been put in serious jeopardy long before the incident in Haslingden baths, when he had written a series of articles for a newspaper. Not only had they been composed without Granada's permission, they also contained very unkind and damaging criticisms of the programme and cast. In writing them, Peter was in serious breach of his contract, which stated that press statements could only be made with the express approval of Granada's management. Knowing we would never agree to the story, Peter went ahead and published without it.

Friends felt betrayed, and the matter could not be allowed to go unpunished. It was decided to suspend him for six weeks without pay, which, if nothing else, meant that he would make little or no profit from the articles. But before the suspension could be put into effect, Peter was arrested, and his breach of contract paled into insignificance beside the police charges.

As far as I was concerned, it was now a time for support. His suspension was set aside, and at Peter's request he was written out of the series while he concentrated on the preparation of his defence.

Legal aid was refused and Peter knew he faced the possibility of an enormous bill from his solicitors. He turned to Granada for help. A £10,000 loan cheque was issued, and was about to be handed over, when Peter admitted, to management's utter disbelief, that he had signed another unauthorised contract to sell his memoirs. It came as no surprise to me.

The question of suspension had for the moment been swept to one side, although it was not forgotten. He had treated Granada's house rules on press interviews with contempt, and if his contract was to be renewed, I wanted firm assurances that this would never happen again. We had a tense meeting, at which he categorically refused to give that promise. From then on I knew that, whatever the outcome of the court case, Len Fairclough's days were numbered.

I had held out an olive branch and

Peter had thrown it back in my face.

Why he found it impossible to give me an undertaking that there would be no repetition of the offensive articles, I am still at a loss to understand. Perhaps the agreement for the next series of revelations had already been signed. Whatever the circumstances, Peter must have realised that he was committing professional suicide and as far as Coronation Street was concerned, there could be no road back. The story he subsequently wrote was unforgivable. No matter what he thought of the Street or its cast, the programme had given him wealth in the good times, and a great deal of loyalty in the bad.

In return for that, his final words were: 'I can't give you any promises. Do what you like.'

Then he turned on his heel and left. That was the last time I saw him. Much later he accused me of not having the courage to sack him face to face. He himself made that impossible by taking a holiday in Bali when Granada sealed his fate. We had no alternative but to put the decision in writing and mail it to his home.

The only question remaining was how Len would be written out of the show. At a scriptwriters' meeting, it was agreed that not only would Len die in a motor-way crash, but it would happen as he returned home from an affair he had been having behind Rita's back.

Of course the public saw this as another twist of the knife, and Peter traded on their sympathy. He had been a professional actor long enough to realise that if a character of Len's fame was to be killed off, the sacrifice would only be made with the help of the most dramatic story-line possible. Instead he chose to believe that Coronation Street had taken revenge for his shame.

Ena Sharples (played by Violet Carson) sheds the famous hairnet for the Queen

15
'THE CURSE OF CORONATION STREET'

If the seed was ever sown for a rich harvest of myth and legend, it was the seed which produced the little potted plant Noel Dyson bought for the cast as a farewell present. Noel played Ida Barlow, Ken's mum, in the earliest days, and although Ida's wasn't the Street's first death, it was the first to be packed with drama and tragedy. Noel never had any intention of making a career out of the fledgling series, despite its early signs of success and, when it came time to say goodbye, she specifically asked for an irrevocable end, involving anything but a heart attack.

The writers, with her blessing, rather cruelly arranged for her to fall under a bus. Millions shared in the sadness. But while the nation mourned and sent wreaths, Noel happily skipped town leaving a little climbing grape-ivy plant as a tangible memorial of her time with the Street.

She could never have guessed how permanent that memorial was to become. Like Topsy, the plant 'just growed'. So did the legend which now surrounds it. Quite who was originally responsible for dreaming up the story has long been forgotten, but that plant became as important to Coronation Street as the ravens are to the Tower of London. The belief grew that if the plant ever died, so would the series. The cast cheerfully seized on the myth. Theatre and television folk are steeped in superstition and from the moment that plant was bestowed with the awesome responsibility of keeping their mortgages paid, ladies of the cast lavished care and attention upon it.

It repaid their kindness and flourished, and the programme blossomed with it. It crept up the walls of the green room and travelled relentlessly across the ceiling. It became known as 'Dear Quatermass'. During an electricians' strike which put us off the air for a time, Pat Phoenix was one of a well-organised band of strike-breakers who slipped past the picket lines to make sure the plant was watered.

When it was decided that the rehearsal and green rooms should be moved, the only real concern was for the health and safety of what was now affectionately called 'Dear Old Quatermass'. After great deliberation it was decided to risk the journey. In a kid-glove operation, and with immense ceremony, the creeper was tenderly carried down two flights of stairs and along to its new home at the other end of the building. The new rehearsal area was altogether more pleasant; larger, lighter and brighter. Dear Old Quatermass throve even better. There were more facilities for the artists, too. For the first time there was enough space in the green room for the actors and actresses to have their own little cubicles, where they could hide away at their desks to learn lines or answer fan mail.

There are all sorts of theories why the artists' rest area in the theatre or studios is called the green room, none particularly satisfactory. Green is historically the colour of bad luck in the profession. Green rooms are never painted green, but the name sticks.

Our bad luck came when we moved green room for a second time. Granada studios were growing at a tremendous pace, and to fit the administration offices into the main building, our band were pushed out into the cold. We were banished to a rehearsal area created from the old goods-yard stable block of the neighbouring Liverpool Street railway station. Viewers would have recognised the outside of the building as the Graffiti Club where Alec Gilroy originally held court, but if Dear Old Quatermass seemed content enough with its third home, the cast were far from happy.

The space available was never adequate, and with everyone packed on top of each other we had the perfect recipe, and mixing bowl, to create a dish of unhappiness. In a desperate attempt to create a few extra feet, a hole was knocked through one wall of the building and some of the male members of cast set up home in a portable cabin on the outside. It was anything but satisfactory. Then, what at first was put down to a run of bad luck began to chisel away at morale. There were illnesses, car crashes, divorces and deaths – in our blackest moments it seemed that our luck had finally run out. There were periods when even the plant looked unhappy and dead leaves were seen as omens of doom. Jean Alexander, a talented and enthusiastic gardener, devoted even more attention to its welfare.

Some seriously thought they had found the answer to our troubles when mystical ley lines were discovered to cross at the very spot where the cast spent so much time. The ancient belief in these channels of power involves the theory that where they cross is a powder keg for an explosion of fortune or misfortune. Stonehenge stands at a crossroads, as does Glastonbury.

In the case of Coronation Street, there were no prizes for guessing which end of the scales of fortune we were being weighed in at. It was all bad news. The press loved it, and the 'Curse of Coronation Street' became a stock headline. Some of the cast took the ley-line theory very seriously. Bill Roache, who had studied various forms of mysticism, and was once a student of the druids, insisted it should be given serious thought, and welcomed a ley-line expert on a conducted tour of the Street's trouble spots. He concluded that great forces were indeed at work, and not for the good. At least we had an independent opinion that our misfortunes were beyond our own control, which, for some, provided a grain of comfort.

Others, including myself, were bemused. In lighter moments, I considered making Ken Barlow a druid. Bill, dressed in the long white robes of the ancient religion, cut a ludicrously entertaining figure. Those who were not laughing openly stood back in amazement. I could just see Ken bringing Coronation Street to a standstill in such clothes. I tried to picture Annie Walker's face when he walked into the Rovers. All kinds of mischief went through my mind. After all, Ken was the Street's great thinker and I could hardly imagine Jack Duckworth taking an interest in paganism. But as our troubles weighed heavier, the temptation passed.

During this period we certainly seemed to be having more than our share of bad luck, and some great sadness too. The lovely Violet Carson died, although it was some time since she had been seen in the programme. Doris Speed's health finally broke down after burglars ransacked her home as she slept, and the wonderful Annie Walker was never seen in the Rovers again. Peter Dudley died. Tragedy followed tragedy. The death of Bernard Youens broke all our hearts and plunged the nation into mourning for the workshy and shiftless Stan Ogden. Jack Howarth died too. Coronation Street had seen the last of Uncle Albert Tatlock.

It all gave weight to the theory of ley lines, and the curse. Doom merchants theorised that, sooner rather than later, the skids would be under the programme itself. While some searched for a deeper meaning for our prevailing sadness, I preferred to content myself with very happy memories of Ena Sharples, Albert Tatlock, Bert Tilsley and Annie Walker, who had given pleasure to millions.

Ena was the last surviving member of the wasp-tongued trinity who dominated the Rovers' snug in the early years. Martha Longhurst had long gone, and Margot Bryant, who played Minnie Caldwell, was just too old to carry on. Over its history Coronation Street has produced some great double acts. Jack

The terrible three — Minnie, Ena and Martha in the snug

and Annie Walker were a perfect match, and Hilda and Stan created the most extraordinarily successful partnership. But never has there been a treble act to match Ena and company, and the killing of Martha is still one of the great mysteries.

She fell in what has been described as the 'great purge' of 1964 when, triggered by a sudden fall in viewing figures, a number of well known faces disappeared from the Street. For the first time in three years, the show had ceased to be Britain's favourite. Steptoe and Son had driven their horse and cart to the top of the ratings and it must have been thought that Martha could be sacrificed for a story that might make them number one again.

It is still talked about today as the Street's greatest mistake; outrageous to have let it happen. Here were three richly contrasting characters who worked beautifully together. To kill one off for a dramatic story-line was ridiculous. I would never have done it. It would be tantamount to killing off Hilda Ogden just to win a brief period with an extra few thousand viewers. When you have gold in your hand, you don't throw it away.

Perhaps the saddest part of it all is that Lynne Carol is still very much alive and well, and could walk back into the Street any time she was invited. Following the death of Margot Bryant, who played Minnie so brilliantly, Lynne and I appeared on a BBC Open Air programme which paid tribute to her career. We talked seriously of the possibility of Lynne coming back in the guise of Martha's twin, who had been living in Australia. If they can get away with dream sequences in Dallas which bring Bobby Ewing back from the dead, I'm sure we could have made Lynne's return

quite credible.

I'm convinced no one in the higher echelons of Granada Television knew of the plans to kill off Martha before it was too late. How it was kept so quiet I can't imagine. Apparently it was discussed with no one other than the writers, and I have never understood how they allowed it to happen.

Had I been making a decision of that magnitude, I would certainly have discussed it at the highest levels, if only to check my own sanity. Even Lynne didn't know until a few days before she was expected to keel over in the snug with a heart attack, and then only because someone leaked a story to the press. She first read of it in her morning newspaper, and it was only confirmed when she was handed a script. Like everyone else in the cast, she was dreadfully upset. Peter Adamson deliberately put in a long pause when Len had to tell everyone else in the Rovers that Martha had died over a milk stout. He prayed sanity might prevail, that Martha would make a recovery, and left the gap so that his announcement could easily be cut from the recording.

Vi Carson was as upset as anyone but like everyone else, she felt helpless, and could only stand back and watch as a trio, unique in television, was cut away. Violet would never have made a fuss. She might quietly have told someone of her disapproval, but that would have been that. She was always a very strait-laced lady, and the complete professional. She hated time-wasting and took the view that everyone called to the studio was there to work, not to waste time enjoying themselves. It was a highly professional attitude, but I think when people are thrown together week after week, year after year, unless there is a fair degree of humour ringing around, they may well go mad.

Even though Vi wouldn't have shared my view, she was held in respect, even awe, by everyone. She was certainly the best-known character the Street ever produced. If Elsie Tanner was the Street's glamorous Queen, Ena Sharples was indisputably the all-powerful matriarch. She was at the core of the programme, and epitomised its essential gritty northern toughness.

All the original characters were wonderfully drawn by Tony Warren, and brilliantly cast. It is remarkable to have found twenty characters who worked so perfectly the first time. Nowadays we struggle to introduce a new family; to find the right mum, dad and two kids is almost impossible. They managed to cast a whole programme and get every character right.

Ena was in fact the last character on the scene. She was always envisaged as a scrawny, thin-faced woman with a tongue like a whip, but when the role proved impossible to fill, Tony Warren recalled Vi from a meeting years before, when Violet was Wilfred Pickles's pianist on the Have a Go show. More or less despairing of casting the part, Coronation Street offered Vi an audition.

She broke all the rules and ignored everything the director had told her about the character. But when she did her own thing at the audition, everyone realised how perfect she was for the part, despite being physically far removed from the figure they had imagined. Vi put her stamp on the proceedings and created the character whose hairnet and old coat became the most famous battledress in Britain.

In many ways, Violet was the odd one out. Margaret Morris, the casting director, later the programme's first woman producer, had been given definite instructions to cast unknowns. It was felt that famous faces would detract from the serial's quest for northern realism. Violet Carson was to be the exception. Her voice was famous on radio, and millions of children knew her as 'Aunty Vi' of Children's Hour. By the time she arrived on Granada's doorstep, Vi was ready to jump ship. She rightly argued that she had given the BBC a lifetime of service and never sold them short. Her rewards had been anything but great. 'They could be, how shall we say, very mean with the pennies,' she complained later. By comparison, the salary Granada offered Violet placed her in what she described as clover.

Violet was wonderful to work with, though she had no great sense of fun. She didn't suffer fools gladly – in fact rarely suffered them at all. But she was superbly professional. Ena was still puppet-mistress of the snug although Martha had long gone even before the early period when I occasionally took over as director. Sometimes Albert Tatlock took over Martha's empty seat and I'll never forget one scene in which he joined the two ladies.

I had prepared a camera script which mapped out where I wanted the three to be seated and called Vi, Margot and Jack over to show them their places. They could get very upset if they were called by their character names, but on this occasion it was the seating arrangements which upturned the apple-cart.

'I can't possible sit there,' Vi announced, in a tone which silenced the whole studio. 'This is my seat. I've sat in it for so many years I can't possibly change now.'

It would have taken a brave man to have stood up to Ena, and I wasn't going

Queen Victoria and Elizabeth I and company greet their subjects in the Street's Jubilee pageant

to attempt to persuade her to move. I resigned myself to rearranging the whole scene. As in a real-life pub, the seats of the regulars are sacrosanct and neither Ena, Minnie or Albert would ever have felt comfortable enough to act their parts in any other position.

As a character actress, Vi was incredible, and with Doris Speed at her side, she once turned in a devastating performance in a very different role from her usual. To celebrate the Queen's Silver Jubilee, Coronation Street devised a float depicting Great Britain through the ages. Bet Lynch sat resplendent as Britannia, Fred Gee dressed as Sir Francis Drake,

Ernie Bishop became Sir Walter Raleigh, and Ken Barlow and Uncle Albert cut an adventurous dash as Everest conquerors Sir Edmund Hillary and Sherpa Tensing. They all looked wonderful, but the Oscars had to go to Annie and Ena.

Annie was superb as Queen Elizabeth I but Ena's Queen Victoria was so lifelike it drew gasps even from the production crew. When these two great Queens strode towards each other from either end of Coronation Street, I think they created a little piece of history all of their own.

When I joined as producer, Ena was getting older, and finding it harder and harder to raise the energy to travel from her Blackpool home. Often she stayed at the Midland Hotel, as did Jack Howarth. But as the years went by, Vi found it increasingly difficult to memorise her lines. Once she actually dried in the middle of a film-take. It came as such a blow to her professional pride she actually cried. Vi fiercely defended her privacy, and to watch someone of her stature and dignity being reduced to tears of frustration was doubly sad.

At one period she didn't appear in the show for over a year, just stayed quietly at her home on the Fylde Coast. Black-pool adored her. But much to Vi's annoyance, the house she shared with her sister became as great a landmark as the Tower. Coach companies even scheduled the quiet semi as a stop on their sightseeing tours.

Had it been me, I would have secretly moved away. Vi was built of sterner stuff. Tired of opening her curtains to stare down on coachloads of trippers, she simply turned her house back to front and spent her remaining years of semi-retirement overlooking the peace of her back garden.

Alec Gilroy and Bet Lynch successfully replaced Annie and Jack Walker as the Rovers' sparring landlords

16

OUR IMMORTALS

Dear Old Quatermass had an advantage over dear old Ena. When the plant became so old and straggly the cast began to fear for its life, a tiny cutting was taken from one of its healthier shoots and to this day the son of Quatermass guards the life of the world's longest-running television show.

I doubt whether any plant could have enjoyed more loving care than ours had from Jean Alexander, whose own name for it was Ermyntrude. But it is now the responsibility of a professional crew of garden experts. They tend all the plants in the splendid, spacious bonded warehouse adjoining the main studios where Coronation Street thankfully set up home after ley lines and acute overcrowding finally drove us from the stables.

If only we could have taken a cutting from Ena. No programme can last for ever, and I really did fear that when the old battle-axe hung up her hairnet, Coronation Street would feel her loss so deeply it might easily start on a downhill slide.

I was very thankful Violet Carson chose to make an exit as gentle as her nature. Her health and strength failed gradually, and in the final years she appeared less and less frequently. There were long periods when Ena was only referred to. But while her face was missing, other people were building a strength of character to fill the immense gap she left. As Vi drifted gracefully away we never seemed to feel the full sense of her loss.

Around this time, I was often nagged by doubts about whether the programme could sustain the loss of its great mainstay characters. Somehow it always did. I found it hard to imagine the Rovers without Annie Walker; I thought the pub would collapse. But then we made Bet Lynch the landlady and now, with Alec Gilroy at her side, we have a beautifully balanced 'odd couple', a duo to rival Jack and Annie. I was long convinced the show could never do without Jean Alexander; but Jack and Vera Duckworth were waiting in the wings to take over where Stan and Hilda left off.

Percy Sugden wears Albert Tatlock's flat cap as the character everyone loves to hate. But the true strength of all these newcomers is their own distinct originality. They are far from clones of the departed. They may have successfully slipped into other folks' shoes, but they have all created fresh and exciting identities.

Percy is as prickly and abrasive as old Albert was tetchy, there is just enough similarity to make the comparison. But there it stops. Both took on the job of a school crossing patrol, but whereas for Albert it was merely a job for an old man trying to eke out his pension, for Percy

Hilda and Rommel – so christened to get Percy's goat

the uniform is a battle-dress and the pole a badge of pride. They even view the wars in quite contrasting ways. Albert rarely confessed the courage which won his chest of medals, while Monty would surely have lost his desert campaigns without the bold Percy at his side. One of my all-time favourite lines was Percy's classic remark: 'When you've made gravy under gunfire, you can do anything.' It was because of Percy's misplaced pride in his wartime exploits that we christened Hilda's cat Rommel. We knew it would get right up the old campaigner's nose.

Like old war horses, cats have to fade away one day. When I took charge of the Street its opening sequence niggled me. The quick-changing views over the slated rooftops of Salford, where the imaginary Weatherfield is supposedly set, seemed to be out of time with the slow, haunting refrains of Eric Spear's signature tune.

I asked to see all the sequence film, shot years before in the backstreets of Old Trafford and Lower Broughton. Although much of it lay on the cutting-room floor, it was reassembled into a continuous film. Suddenly, on walked that wonderful cat. When it curled up in the spring sunshine I knew I had found the perfect clip. It looked exactly as though it had contentedly sat down to watch the programme, and from that day the Coronation Street cat became almost as famous as any character on the show. It provided us with an enduring mystery, too. Any number of people, impostors all, insisted they were the owners, but its true identity was never discovered.

On the eve of my retirement, the Street's new production team agreed that the opening titles needed to be slightly updated yet again. Perhaps it will develop into a tradition and become the first sweep of every new broom. But as a parting shot, I reminded them there would be a national outcry if a cat wasn't included somewhere. At the time of writing I'm still wondering how they will persuade their new star-struck moggie to act as naturally as the original.

The last time the programme was faced with finding a stand-in ginger tom, we somehow managed to hoodwink the fans. I was walking along the corridor one morning when I was greeted by a tearful Margot Bryant. Minnie Caldwell's cat Bobby had died, and although we managed to find a replacement without a single viewer spotting the switch, Margot appeared genuinely distraught. I would have expected Minnie to be deeply upset, but the real Margot Bryant was an abrasively tough lady not usually given to tears, and far removed from sweet little old Minnie Caldwell. She may have had a weakness for cats, and Bobby in particular, but that was one of the few chinks I ever found in Margot's armour.

Her home was in Brighton and years of train travel to and from Manchester had filled her with a deep hatred for British Rail. Margot journeyed up and down each week, and on Mondays, when the cast gathered to begin the week's work, she often had a great deal to say about the shortcomings of BR's network and timing. For them, she reserved the full force of her invective, all delivered in a language so shockingly colourful, no one would have believed it came from sweet lips of Minnie Caldwell. Margot's vocabulary astounded even me at times. She had a way with words which was at times distinctly unladylike, and what's more she couldn't have cared less who happened to be listening.

When the mood took her, she could be just as quarrelsome in the studio as she could be with errant railwaymen. She only ever read her own lines and for the most part I don't think she had a clue what was happening in the rest of the script. One day, called to take her customary seat in the snug, Margot realised she didn't have a line to say. Her patience snapped, and she shouted, 'I don't know why I'm in this scene at all.'

If she had bothered to read the script all would have become clear. But I had to explain patiently that another character, passing through the corner shop a few scenes earlier, had clearly said, 'I've just seen Minnie in the Rovers.' Even so it was difficult to convince Margot why the silent figure of Minnie, nursing a milk stout, had to be seen in a following sequence. As I had had to explain to Pat Phoenix, in the Street even stars have to act as extras sometimes.

When I took over as producer, Margot was well into her seventies and her health was beginning to fail. At one time she had a year out for a complete rest, and when she telephoned to say she was on her way back to the studios, I decided this deserved a little champagne celebration.

As she was due to arrive almost immediately, I asked Gordon McKellar if he could quickly rustle up a bottle. Right on cue Margot turned up, radiant in a powder-blue suit with intricate embroidery around the collar. It was lovely to see her again, and I was complimenting her on how beautiful she looked when Gordon rushed in with the champagne and glasses. Margot sat preening herself as I set about opening the bottle.

Gordon must have run up the stairs shaking it all the way. As I began to untwist the wire, the cork blew out and Margot was drenched in an explosion of champagne. At any other time it might have been funny. I wanted to laugh but felt terrible at the same time. She did her best to smile, but knowing Margot, I'll bet there were some wonderful barrack-room expletives running through her head. Luckily there was just enough champagne left to toast away the tension.

Margot came back for a while, but it became increasingly difficult for her to memorise her lines. She began cutting them from the script and sticking them to the back of her handbag. But when it became obvious to everyone that she was reading during a recording, it had sadly reached the stage where it would have been unfair to ask her to carry on a moment longer. She wasn't at all well. There were more periods of illness, until finally we found her a place in a beautiful Cheshire nursing home where she spent the remainder of her days happily and in comfort.

Doris Speed was another great lady of the theatre who battled along until age finally defeated her. No one really knew quite how old Doris was, and we were as surprised as she was deeply hurt when a newspaper revealed her age, and shamefully published a copy of her birth certificate to authenticate the intrusion. Unknown to anyone at Granada, she had actually retired and was drawing her pension when Annie Walker, with all her towering social pretensions, first held court behind the bar of the Rovers back in 1960. No one dreamt she was in her eighties when she finally succumbed to a stomach illness and never again felt well enough to return to the pub she made so famous.

Annie Walker, a true blue Tory, may have been lost in a make-believe world of her airs and graces. Doris was different. A lifelong socialist, her feet firmly on the ground, she also possessed the most wonderfully cutting sense of humour. Doris lived with her ageing mother, Ada, at their neat, unpretentious semi-detached home in a quiet cul-de-sac in the south Manchester suburb of Chorlton-cum-Hardy. The story is told that one evening the two were watching Coronation Street when Mum turned to her daughter and announced, 'I am eighty-seven years old, but thank God I've never looked as old as you looked tonight.' It was alleged they didn't speak for almost a week.

Not long ago a Rolls Royce was laid on to bring Doris to the studios for a charity telethon, and I went with the chauffeur to collect her. I had always wondered if the story was true, and as we drove to the studios I found the right moment to ask her.

'My dear boy, I'll tell you the whole story,' she said with a smile. 'It's even better.'

Doris explained it was all to do with her eyes. Apparently they seemed to have got lost somewhere under her eye-shadow and she had made a mental note to have stern words with Glenda, the make-up lady who looked after her. The slip-up hadn't escaped Ada's attention either. Doris's mother was actually well into her nineties, but it didn't stop her turning from the screen and saying, 'Doris, if I ever looked as old as you did tonight I'd commit suicide.'

The following morning, Glenda's name was at the top of Doris's calling card.

'Did you see the programme last night?' Doris enquired.

'I did,' Glenda replied, puzzled by the actress's unusually frosty tone.

'Then you will have noticed you couldn't see my eyes. Now it's not on, and I hope you will be doing something about it.'

The make-up artist respectfully accepted her ticking-off in silence. But as Doris lay back to allow the make-up session to start, Glenda looked down and said, 'Doris, in amongst that face there are two eyes, and you're right, it's my job to find them.'

They both roared with laughter and, friendship restored, busied themselves with the hunt.

Doris enjoyed telling the story, though it was against herself. But usually her caustic wit was reserved for the unfortunate who perilously crossed her path.

A wonderfully entertaining story was scripted some years ago when Annie decided her station in life could only be enhanced by the status of owning a Rover car. An actor called Roger Brierley was brought in to play Lanky Potts, the dealer with the motor she coveted.

Roger's height was to cause him problems. He was well over six feet, and when it came to discussing the sale of the car he noticed his towering frame was casting a perhaps unwelcome shadow over the actress. The two were rehearsing their lines before the recording when Roger began to move his head from side to side to see if he could find a position which didn't cast a shadow over Annie's face.

Perplexed, Doris put her hands on his shoulders and scolded, 'Excuse me, dear boy, you won't be dodging from side to side when we do the take, will you? It's very off-putting.'

Roger was full of apology and respectfully explained what he was trying to do. Quick as a flash, Doris looked him in the eye and warned, 'There's a very long dole queue of actors who have cast a shadow on the face of Doris Speed.'

As age slowly crept up, it wasn't surprising that Doris became more nervous of scenes which involved her in large tracts of dialogue. We tried to keep them to a minimum, but one week she was unavoidably involved in a major story-line and found herself carrying half the programme almost single-handed.

She feared her memory might let her down, although I knew she was a lot better at remembering lines than she gave herself credit for. In the event she turned in a magnificent performance. It was so good that I sent out for a bouquet, which I presented as she was leaving for home.

She was overwhelmed. After all her years in showbusiness and, indeed, Coronation Street, she looked at the flowers amazed, and said, 'Do you know, this is the first time ever that anyone has presented me with a bouquet. It's absolutely wonderful and I shall never forget this moment.' What was meant as a little thank you turned quite unexpectedly into a very moving moment.

Jack Howarth was another wonderful character of the Street's old guard. His sense of humour bubbled along despite the crotchety character he played and he adored telling jokes. Jack was a veteran from theatre and radio; for years before joining the Street he had been the voice of Mr Maggs in Mrs Dale's Diary.

Throughout his long career, Jack had rarely been out of work, but in those days the job was far from well paid. Coronation Street salaries must have been like pools wins in comparison, but after years of living down to his frugal wages, Jack was far too set in his ways to become a Flash Harry. Some might say he was tight with his money, but he was a wonderful character and I shall describe him in no unkinder way than thrifty.

He was always at his most entertaining at the Friday lunch which became a Coronation Street tradition. At first we all went to the canteen, because it was the day we filmed the programme and everyone was in make-up and costume, but the cast had to elbow their way through all the other Granada staff wanting a quick bite. Eventually a special buffet was laid on, first in the green room, later in one of the large committee rooms. There was always a splendid spread, and Friday lunch became a very pleasant ritual.

To Jack it must have looked like a throw-back to the old theatre days, when an actor's idea of a good play was one which involved eating a meal on stage. At least it saved the cost of supper. There were always a few tasty left-overs from the buffet and Jack couldn't resist wandering around the tables shamelessly pocketing anything he fancied for a little snack later. As he wore the same suit for twenty years, I hate to think what state the pockets were in. It was just as well the suit was regularly cleaned, or those pockets would have constituted a health hazard.

One Friday a splendid bunch of grapes caught Jack's eye. He carefully split them into two smaller bunches, wrapped them in cling-film and popped them into his pockets. Graham Haberfield, who was always a bit of a joker, watched the whole performance and saw an opportunity too good to be missed.

He greeted Jack like a long-lost uncle, slapped his pockets as hard as he could and shouted, 'My dear fellow, how are you?'

The rest of us roared, but Jack, for once, missed the joke and stomped off huffing and puffing, grape juice dripping as he went.

Jack was married to the former actress,

Annie Walker in full glory as Elizabeth I

Betty Murgatroyd, and had a beautiful home at Deganwy in North Wales. He could not possibly have made the journey daily, so during the week he took a room at the Midland. It was almost a mile from the studios, but Jack looked upon taxis as an unnecessary expense and usually insisted on catching a bus.

A friend of mine was driving past Granada one evening and spotted Jack at the bus stop in the rain. Knowing the old gentleman stayed at the Midland, he offered him a lift. A few minutes later he came to a halt outside Manchester Central Library, directly across the road from the hotel. Jack stayed put in the passenger seat and without a hint of apology asked, 'Do you think you could drop me at the door?'

My friend obliged, steering through the rush-hour traffic. Even that added kindness was not enough for Jack. He was a tireless worker for charity and a vice-president of SOS, the Stars Organisation for Spastics. He spent many summers roaming holiday camps, appearing on stage and embarrassing holidaymakers out of their cash. He wasn't prepared to let an obviously well-to-do businessman off the hook.

'Right,' he announced as he pulled a great wad of raffle tickets from his pocket. 'You'd better buy some of these.'

Jack's colourful character blended in so well with Albert Tatlock's that it would have taken an expert to spot the difference. On the face of it, only Albert's false moustache told them apart. Why Jack didn't just grow one, I never discovered. Perhaps popping a touch of glue on his upper lip was easier than trimming the real thing.

Arthur Lowe, who in the early days of Coronation Street played the pompous little shopkeeper Leonard Swindley, was another actor very careful with his pennies. Once I was rehearsing him through a show called Last of the Baskets when he announced it was a black day for Britain. The price of Rolls Royce shares had collapsed, and poor Arthur appeared to have lost a small fortune. His only crumb of comfort was that his pal Ernie Wise had lost even more.

The following morning I decided to pull Arthur's leg and I told him a Swiss consortium was on the verge of bailing out the beleaguered firm.

'Oh!' said Arthur, sensing an upturn in his financial fortunes. 'What's it all about?'

'They're going to make Swiss Rolls,' I cracked back.

Arthur was not amused. He stomped off muttering darkly, 'Oh, very droll, very droll indeed.'

17

ROMANCE
IN THE AIR

A world of magic-carpet travel unrolled before us one May morning when the Heathrow staff of British Airways' first-class lounge welcomed Julie Goodyear with, 'Good morning, madam, would you care for champagne?'

Julie caught her breath. I'm sure I did too. Brassy Bet Lynch, barmaid of the Rovers, had been awarded platignum-card status for the first time in her life, and just for a moment I think we both sensed a distinct danger that she was about to be bowled over by it.

'No thank you,' said Julie, trying hard to pretend that being offered the finest champagne at ten in the morning was nothing to a star of her status. 'But I would like a brandy.'

We chose from the greatest selection of fine cognacs and malt whiskies I have ever seen on a bar, before being ushered to our waiting jumbo jet.

Every couple of years, New Zealand Television holds a twenty-four-hour charity telethon, and as Coronation Street is one of the country's favourite programmes, Julie and I had been invited to fly the Weatherfield flag. The vision of the aircraft's first-class lounge was enough to stop Julie in her tracks. 'I don't believe this,' she whispered. 'Bill, wake me up, wake me up.'

For two people more accustomed to the knees-under-the-chin discomfort of a holiday charter, the unashamed opu-lence of that cabin was eye-popping.

'It's all true, it's all true,' I kept repeating as the steward sat us down in luxury armchairs, at least four feet apart. For comfort I was travelling in a casual bomber jacket. I was about to bundle it up in an overhead locker when the steward raced to its rescue. It might have been finest cashmere. He gently shook it straight and hung it in a forward ward-robe.

Moments later glasses of champagne were placed in our hands. In economy class you wait until 30,000 feet before they even offer a drink. In first, you ascend skywards trying not to spill the glass. It isn't plastic either, but pure crystal.

Lunch was a mouth-watering array of hors d'oeuvres, followed by a choice between lobster thermidor or roast pheasant in burgundy sauce. I was beginning to suspect this was a dream after all. Any pretence that first-class travel was everyday fare for us was shot to pieces. We just couldn't make up our minds, so the steward suggested, 'Have the lobster to start, and if there's any room left you can have pheasant to follow.' A wonderful idea.

The first leg of the flight was to Los Angeles, by the polar route. As the North Atlantic slipped by five miles below, Julie became fascinated by a man on the opposite side of the cabin, beavering

Julie – the only woman in the world who prefers brandy to champagne! (Photo: Bill Podmore)

away with a file of papers and a personal computer. Eventually Julie said, 'That man hasn't stopped working from the moment he came on board. I'm going to ask him what it's all about.'

'Hello,' she announced holding out her hand. 'I'm Julie.'

'Oh, hello,' he replied, taking his nose out of his paperwork. 'I'm Richard, Richard Skrob.'

'Do you ever stop working?' Julie asked.

'Well, it's a long flight and a day wasted if you do,' was his reply.

Julie was intrigued by the bespectacled Californian she later described as politely old-fashioned, gentle, and quite the kindest man she had ever met. Richard explained he had a home and children in Los Angeles, worked for the

Lockheed Aircraft Corporation, and spent most of his working life jetting around the world as an executive with a particular interest in those little black boxes we hear so much about whenever there is an air crash.

The two of them hit it off from the first. Family photographs came out, they swapped stories about their jobs and lifestyles, and before we descended into LA they were the best of new-found friends.

They had one rather tragic subject in common. Richard revealed that his wife had died of cancer. Nothing could have struck a more sympathetic chord with Julie. She had narrowly escaped death herself from cervical cancer, and still faced a long and agonising wait before being given the all-clear.

Julie and I had a few hours to wait for our onward flight. Richard insisted we come aboard his yacht for drinks. We would have accepted eagerly if an immigration official hadn't spotted that we didn't have American visas and ordered us not to leave the airport.

Richard suggested the perfect compromise. He had some immediate arrangements to look after, but promised to join us for drinks in the Air New Zealand lounge.

I settled down with a magazine, but as the hours passed, I couldn't help noticing that relations between Julie and Richard were developing into something much more than a passing friendship. They had now been locked in conversation for eleven hours solid and, as our flight was called, there was romance in the air and genuine affection in their goodbye kisses. It eventually led to a remarkable transatlantic love affair, crowned by a romantic wedding in Barbados two years later.

At that moment, however, Fiji beckoned. We landed out of the tropical night in one of the most beautiful and romantic spots on earth. The hotel, the Regent of Fiji, was the most breathtakingly exotic place either of us had ever seen. The rooms were enormous and airy, the whole of one wall a patio door to palm-fringed lawns, with the gentle roar of Pacific surf in the background.

It would have been paradise if it hadn't been for a squadron of mosquitoes hell-bent on making a meal of Britain's favourite barmaid. We spent the day by the pool, and as dusk fell I should have realised the dangers when a hotel employee went to work spraying the shrubs on the far side of the pool. We just carried on chatting to a guest we had met earlier, and although we were all flicking away insects, I don't think any of us realised we might be being bitten.

The next morning, Julie called my room. 'You had better come down here and take a look at me.'

She was covered in angry red blotches, but wasn't in any great discomfort, and we went down to breakfast and out to the pool. Two rather nice Australian hairdressers, Garth and Bernard, instantly recognised her. Julie couldn't believe it. Here she was, sat like some castaway on a Pacific island, and still she couldn't escape Bet Lynch.

Julie – blotchy but unbowed (Photo: Bill Podmore)

They looked at Julie's blotches with deepening concern and I went to the hotel chemist for cream to cool the swellings. He announced he had just the ointment and I returned with my little package to the pool.

Julie tore it open and fell about laughing. The ointment was for piles. Little did we realise that that was exactly what was needed. The pile ointment was tossed in a bin and we lazed our way through the day. The pool had a bar, and Julie was persuaded to entertain customers as a tropical Bet Lynch.

That night Fijian warriors and their womenfolk put on a traditional display; my only disappointment. I had expected Fijian women to be stunningly beautiful; sadly, it was almost impossible to tell them from the men. They all wore grass skirts, which further confused the issue.

The next morning, Julie's blotches had swollen into enormous blisters. It was a terrible sight and when a doctor arrived to administer an antihistamine injection, she really was quite poorly. The poison had entered her system. And we faced a further flight, albeit a short one, from Fiji to Auckland.

Julie was recognised by everyone on the plane and all expressed concern. The crew folded down a seat in front so she could sit with her legs outstretched, but by the time we landed in New Zealand she was really ill.

We were met at the airport by Des Moynahan, an ex-Brit, a great guy and the programme controller of New Zealand Television. He took one look at Julie and whisked us to our hotel. Marti Caine, Kenny Everett and Basil Brush arrived and we were all invited to a dinner with the Director General of New Zealand TV.

Julie stayed in bed feeling rather sorry for herself, but next morning she was well enough to travel to Palmerston North where we were based for the telethon. She was never able to take her full part in the show but, ignoring doctor's orders to stay in bed, she managed a couple of slots.

She certainly hadn't lost her sense of humour. At one point Marti Caine offered the dress she was wearing to the highest bidder. Never one to be upstaged, Julie offered her bra.

We flew home with yet another stop-off in Singapore and although Julie struck up a friendship with a handsome member of the aircraft crew, I was sure her heart was thousands of miles away.

Julie hadn't said much about Richard Skrob, except that she found him fascinating. But I didn't doubt that an extraordinary relationship had been building between them. You don't normally spend eleven hours in intimate conversation with a total stranger.

They had made a date to meet at the next Paris air show, but by the time we arrived home he had already called Granada studios and left a message for Julie. I met Richard quite often over the next couple of years. Although he was American, much about his manner was characteristically English. He was always smartly dressed, invariably in blazer and flannels, with a slightly reserved manner, and always immaculately polite.

They married in secret, or at least Julie kept it secret, even from her closest friends in the cast.

She came back from her Christmas honeymoon in Barbados and announced dramatically: 'There's good news and bad news. The good news is I'm proud and happy to tell you I'm now Mrs Richard Skrob. The bad news is I'm staying with the Street.'

Julie had only recently been made

landlady of the Rovers and she added, 'I couldn't let you down just when I've been promoted.'

She had accepted Richard's third marriage proposal, and presented herself with a dilemma. He had offered security and a luxury lifestyle in LA.

'Funny isn't it?' she said later. 'But when it came to a choice, that cobbled street meant more to me than an exclusive American suburb.'

From there it all seemed to go sadly wrong. Julie could never give up Coronation Street and he couldn't give up his high-powered job roaming the world. You can't hope to have a marriage on those terms.

Julie never confided the details, but the final break-up must have been heartbreaking for them both. She would only say that it hadn't worked out, and even she didn't really know what went wrong.

It was a strange marriage and one which I thought doomed from the start. Coronation Street was really everything Julie ever wanted; I don't think anyone or anything could have tempted her away from it.

Julie Goodyear is the Queen of the Soaps. There has been a dynasty of them throughout the life of Coronation Street, But Julie has all the glitz and glam to keep her wearing the crown for a long, long time.

Early years in the RAF have prepared Bill Podmore for the life of a seasoned jet-setter (Photo: Bill Podmore)

18

THE FEAR
OF FLYING

The eighteenth-century English clergyman Augustus Toplady left an enduring memorial, though he died aged only thirty-eight. The opening lines of his hymn, 'Rock of ages cleft for me, Let me hide myself in thee' are always moving. When sung with the fervour of one convinced they are about to meet their Maker, they swell with even greater richness. At three thousand feet in a lost aircraft with its fuel-gauge needles banging against the empty stops, Pat Phoenix must have been feeling close indeed to the Almighty, and burst into song.

I could hardly blame her. The outlook from the four-seater Cessna must, in her eyes, have appeared bleak. Having trained as a pilot, I at least understood the danger we were in. It wasn't quite as hopeless as Pat imagined, although as the minutes ticked by I was becoming increasingly worried. If the seemingly inevitable crash landing happened, I had the co-pilot's controls to hang on to, and some guiding hand in our destiny. In the rear seat, all Pat had to cling to were the last drops of celebration champagne and her firm faith in God to balance her decreasing trust in a perplexed pilot.

The day had begun wonderfully. Pat and her business manager, Keith Pollit, had somehow managed to double-book a Saturday personal appearance, but had solved the problem of how to be in Cardiff and Crewe within a couple of hours by chartering a light aircraft. Flying is my idea of heaven, and when Pat called to say there would be a spare seat, I didn't need to be asked twice.

We took off from Manchester in perfect weather and thoroughly enjoyed a near cloudless flight to Cardiff. Pat had been contracted to add a touch of Coronation Street glamour to an entrepreneur's new venture, organising one-day markets at venues throughout the country. Cardiff had been chosen on this particular Sunday, and a Rolls Royce was at the airport to whisk us into the city centre. Our hosts laid on a splendid Welsh welcome with cheering crowds and an open-topped vintage car in which to tour the market.

Everything was running to schedule and Keith even found a moment to buy a bottle of champagne to toast our success on the return flight to Crewe. The plan was to land at an old RAF airstrip just outside Whitchurch and drive the last ten miles to open an electronic bingo arcade in Crewe centre.

The destination was little more than an hour's flying time at a leisurely one hundred miles an hour, the only blot on the horizon a newly arrived belt of thick cloud. Our cruising height committed us to flying almost blind, but Pat and Keith were contented enough with their champagne, while I took an interest in the electronic gadgetry which, according to the pilot, would take us with pin-point accuracy from one radio beacon to the next as we flew north.

I had once lost myself on a low-level navigational exercise in Rhodesia, and very unnerving it was. Navigation was a lot less sophisticated then, and the rather ancient Harvard I was flying was no match for the modern Cessna. I very nearly came to grief, despite having been assessed as above average in navigation skills, and all because I forgot the basic navigational principle that magnetic north of a compass bearing is always a few degrees different from true north. Over a long distance, that principle has real significance. There were no marks for me on that training flight, and only black ones could be awarded to the pilot of our Cessna.

On this flight, radio beacons had been our supposedly infallible guide and at the appropriate moment we began our descent. As we broke through the cloud base the pilot identified the town below as Whitchurch and confidently announced that in a few minutes we would touch down at the airstrip we were heading for. An air map folded on his knee, he had but to follow the railway line for a few minutes, then make a left turn.

We followed the line, made the necessary course corrections, but below was nothing but fields. Our pilot studied his map again and made another circle of the countryside searching for a strip of concrete. The search became increasingly frantic as we flew in ever-widening circles for the next thirty minutes. Eventually the pilot was forced to admit he hadn't a clue where we were. We were hopelessly lost, and getting more lost with every spiral. Keith and Pat began to find the solace of their rapidly emptying bottle inadequate. I wasn't exactly frightened, but I was beginning to think we might have to make a forced landing in a field.

Our aircraft was now well overdue and air traffic control at Cardiff had sent out an alert. Our flight plan and estimated time of arrival had been logged. In the absence of any report of our whereabouts, they had rightly concluded that if we were still in the air our tanks must be nearly empty. Manchester air traffic control had been brought into the alert but as we buzzed around looking for an non-existent airstrip with the worry lines cutting deeper and deeper, we didn't hear a word of the radio messages organising a full-scale search. The emergency alert apparently stated that the plane was carrying VIPs – namely Miss Pat Phoenix and her party. Since we had sent no message, distress or otherwise, the authorities feared we had either crashed, force-landed, or simply disappeared into some Welsh version of the Bermuda Triangle.

By this time the pilot was more than willing to share his responsibility and readily agreed to let me look at his air map. I studied the contours of the land below. There wasn't a great deal to go on but I spotted a range of hills to the left, and with the pilot's blessing made these the starting point for fresh calculations. We soon came up with an acceptable answer to our troubles.

The town we had spotted could not have been Whitchurch. We must have made our descent twenty miles too early, and based our search for the airstrip on Shrewsbury. We identified a main road heading north from the town which should lead to Whitchurch. My main worry was that both fuel gauges read empty.

'Don't worry,' said the pilot, 'I know

those gauges. There's always something in the tanks, even when they read rock bottom.'

I was not filled with confidence. Pat's only answer was to sing her favourite hymn; Keith joined in. Pat told me later that she was quite sure we were all going to die.

I did my best to keep up her courage. 'These little planes glide along even when all the fuel has gone,' I said, with as much conviction as I could muster. 'If the engine conks out, we will just glide down. There are plenty of fields to land in.' From two thousand feet, it hardly sounded convincing.

Whitchurch, or what we were praying was Whitchurch, came into view, and so did the railway line. We followed it for a few minutes and made our final turn. If we were wrong this time, a crash landing was inevitable. I was searching for a suitable site when the airstrip came into sight.

I have never been so pleased to see a strip of bare concrete. The runway was neglected, with grass growing between the slabs. But there was a light plane parked alongside one end and a windsock streaming in the breeze, so I assumed it was still in service.

We swung round for our final approach and from a height of a few hundred feet the pilot announced, 'I don't like the look of this. It's a bit rough.'

I didn't like to argue with the man at the controls but from where I was sitting, that ribbon of grey looked just wonderful. 'Let's just thank God we found it,' said I. 'Now, shall we put this bloody thing down?'

He decided to attempt the slowest approach possible to save damaging the undercarriage on the rough ground. Halfway through the descent, the stall buzzer screeched a warning. My shout of alarm must have been even louder. I'm prepared to debate that a Cessna 172's built-in safety and balance factors are such that, left to its own devices, it might pull out of a stall. But it's one of those debates I would prefer to have in the safety of a pub. With the full weight of four people on board I was not prepared to take part in an experiment.

With seconds to spare, the pilot correctly dropped the nose to gather enough speed to prevent us falling into a spin and with a final burst of engine power made a most thankful touchdown.

Pat, shaken and pale, crossed herself and was still saying Hail Marys as we drove into Crewe. We were in no mood for bingo, but somehow Pat managed a brave smile and I very much doubt that the cheering crowds guessed how close we had come to losing their soap Queen.

Though they look like the best of friends, Chris Quinten's open defiance of a Coronation Street ruling nearly cost him the part of Brian (Photo: Bill Podmore)

19

THE RULES –
HOW NOT TO BREAK THEM

Whether to make personal appearances is a decision left entirely to individual cast members. Some make a healthy second income from opening shops and turning up to support events as wide-ranging as golf tournaments and village fêtes. Others, with a perhaps more altruistic outlook, lend their names and faces solely to charity work. But what the actors and actresses choose to do in public is governed to a great extent by a minefield of rules, some imposed by Granada, but many of the more important laid down by the strict code of the Independent Broadcasting Authority.

Perhaps the most important of these concerns advertising. No one must appear in a television commercial or be seen on the screen endorsing a product or service while appearing in a show which the viewers might align to it. This rule is tightly enforced.

An artist appearing in any programme, whether a one-off play or a lengthy series, is not allowed to appear in the advertising breaks during or around the show's transmission time.

In a twice-weekly series as high-profile as Coronation Street, this completely rules out the possibility of our stars signing what might be a very lucrative advertising contract. One of the first things Street newcomers are asked is to declare their current, or even past, advertising tie-ups.

Guidelines on advertising, or what might be seen as advertising, are even applied to personal appearance work. Julie Goodyear is free to lend her name to a commercial venture, but I'm afraid Bet Lynch isn't. It is not a rule diligently policed these days; nevertheless, it is there, and on one occasion I was given a good dressing-down as the producer who unwittingly allowed it to be broken.

Some years ago Peter Adamson was asked to open a large do-it-yourself centre in Birmingham. Naturally enough, the organisers couldn't resist the temptation to give maximum publicity not to Peter, but to Len Fairclough. Within forty-eight hours I had my wrists slapped in a very stern letter from the IBA.

These restrictions, perhaps a little unfairly, apply only to artists currently under contract to the independent channels. Our BBC colleagues have the advantage here. No one could stand in the way of Terry Wogan telling us of the wonders of his favourite brand of margarine, but woe betide Betty Turpin if she appeared on the box enthusing over someone else's hotpot, or Vera Duckworth championing the finer points of stone cladding.

There was a time when the IBA watchdogs kept an eagle eye on the products used in TV programmes. If an actor had to pour out a scotch they preferred it to

Studio view of the corner shop before its 'expansion' into Alf's Mini Market

come from an anonymous decanter. If a bottle had to be used, then the label must be covered by his hand, or at least held out of camera shot. Stocking our corner shop was a nightmare. There was a long period when we invented brand names for all the products on sale, and our props department was asked to create new packaging for almost everything on the shelves. If brand-name products went on display, the name had to be blotted out. For instance, the word Kelloggs`had to be blacked out from a cornflake packet, even though the cockerel logo was an absolute giveaway. It was only with the advent of colour television that the rulings started to be relaxed. A black band hiding a name such as Kelloggs only drew attention to the packet, so instead it was decreed that brand-names could be used as long as no one product was given precedence.

In the changeover period mistakes were bound to be made and manufacturers as well as viewers were quick to spot them. Quite by accident, the shop happened to display an assortment of Jacobs biscuits. It wasn't long before another major manufacturer, Crawfords, drew our attention to what they saw as unfair competition, and left us with no option but to give their products an equal display. But we dropped our biggest clanger when Co-op products suddenly appeared in Alf's shop. A puzzled viewer wrote to me saying that Co-op brands, with their distinctive logo, were normally only to be found in Co-op shops. I pointed this out to the props department, and for a while they would disappear. Of course, a few weeks later, when my request had been forgotten, the tins would annoyingly reappear. I only solved the problem when, tired of making polite requests, I ordered the whole Co-op stock destroyed.

As producer of Coronation Street, a serial which despite all our efforts will no doubt continue to be referred to as a 'soap opera', I have complete sympathy with any efforts to keep commercial interests out of programme-making.

The term 'soap opera' derives from the rash of radio programmes created many years ago in America by soap manufacturers such as Procter and Gamble to sponsor their products. At one time sixty-odd of these programmes were being transmitted, and later they crept into television as well.

The tag became synonymous with badly-produced, poorly-written, under-rehearsed, low-budget trash. Although I have grown to accept that the name will always be pegged on long-running series like the Street, it still infuriates me.

Coronation Street is anything but a programme knocked off in a hurry. A great deal of care and detailed attention is lavished on its production, and it would never have survived the last three decades, and held its spot so high in the ratings, without it. It is a drama series – superbly written and beautifully acted – and I wish television pundits would call it that. Once, during a television interview on 'soap', I said I was prepared to tolerate the phrase 'folk opera' – a much better description.

Very recently, Granada has softened slightly in its attitude to cast members doing other work, but during my time, the company forbade them from appearing in any other programmes whilst contracted to the show. That only applied to television, however. I was happy to try and meet any request from an artist wishing to be written out in order to appear in the theatre.

It isn't everyone's cup of tea. Some

among the Street's cast, who lack experience of the live theatre, would probably run a mile from any suggestion that they try their hand at a stage play.

Thelma Barlow, who is wonderful as the delightfully dizzy Mavis Riley, was not long ago written out for a few weeks with my blessing and won rave reviews for her part in a Chekhov play. On the other hand, although I can think of no one finer than Julie Goodyear to play Bet Lynch, I can't imagine her wanting to attempt theatre.

When the occasional request came from a member of the cast wanting to have a shot at theatre, I would put a fatherly arm around their shoulders and warn that appearing on stage every night, with matinees thrown in on Wednesdays and Saturdays, was very gruelling work, and a world away from the comparatively leisurely pace of Coronation Street. Some listened, others didn't.

For those who can handle the work, I can think of nothing finer than a new experience spreading their wings in a different arena. It must be a breath of fresh air after being closeted for months, even years, in the guise of a Coronation Street character. But even those from a theatre background often forgot just how hard the life was.

The programme never had a finer actress than Jean Alexander, and long before I became producer she took off for a while to appear in a production of *Arsenic and Old Lace*. She returned to the comforting arms of Stan, a worn-out and wiser woman, complaining, 'I just don't know why I did it. I've done my apprenticeship in the theatre and why I ever wanted to go back, I'll never know.'

Johnny Briggs was pretty much the same. He once sallied forth, full of enthusiasm, to play a detective in Priest-ley's *An Inspector Calls*. The play was going on tour, and I was sure Johnny had no idea what a strain that could be.

'Doing matinees too?' I enquired, when he came to get permission to quit the Street for a while.

'Yes,' he replied in a voice soaked in delight.

'You'll hate it,' I solemnly warned.

'No I won't. I'm looking forward to it.'

'Off you go then. I'll write you out for eight weeks.'

Two months later he dragged himself back into the studios, saying, 'Bill, I promise I'll listen to you in the future. My God I wish I'd taken some notice of what you said. It was such hard work, I couldn't believe it.'

Johnny Briggs never did theatre again. You really do earn your money in that game, and even when you are a star, the financial rewards by no means match the effort needed to climb to the top.

Pat Phoenix, of course, loved every moment of it and it was the stage which lured her away on the two occasions she turned her back on Coronation Street. She would wrap the grease paint and the glamour around her like a fox-fur stole. On the other hand, it was mink she came back for. I've always believed it was the need for cash and security that drove her back to Coronation Street soon after I joined.

Lynne Perrie also loves performing before a live audience. Her meat is cabaret; personal appearances run a close second. Lynne enjoys it all so much, I'm surprised she doesn't pay her hosts for the pleasure of taking part. She is a great extrovert character with a wonderful singing voice which seems all the more remarkable in so slight a frame. When that lady sings with all her heart, she can really belt it out.

Taking a few weeks away for work in

the theatre was one thing, but I did finally draw the line at pantomime. The great attraction of a Christmas show is the pay cheque. Big-name performers are handsomely rewarded. Coronation Street stars come even higher in the pay scale. Under Granada's rules, the artists could only be billed under their own names, never their characters'. Few took a blind bit of notice. There was too much money at stake for promoters and theatre managements to ignore the crowd-pulling power of billing Len Fairclough or Eddie Yeats.

But that wasn't why I was forced to put an end to the great little money spinner. One year, to my horror, I discovered during a story-planning conference that four of our male leads had been released to appear in pantomime. There was no one to blame but me. At different times of the year they had all come seeking permission, and in each case I had foolishly agreed, without realising how great a hole I was creating in the programme. Coronation Street has always been a matriarchal society but at that period men were particularly thin on the ground. Now we faced a Christmas and New Year with four leading men missing. It was hard enough dreaming up fresh story-lines month after month with every cast member available. But when Len Fairclough, Eddie Yeats, Alf Roberts and Fred Gee all went off to play Aladdin or Mother Goose, the writers were far from happy.

The rule-book had to be rewritten, as it could never be allowed to happen again. Unfortunately, to be fair the rules had to apply to everyone. More than a handful were upset by the panto ban, but the majority of the cast appreciated the reasoning behind my decision.

Rules, of course, are there to be broken and Chris Quinten was the first bold

enough to see if he could climb the barbed wire. He came to me bubbling over with excitement after being offered a very lucrative contract to star in a Christmas panto at Lincoln. I listened patiently, and explained at length why there could be no rule-bending, but Chris was far from happy. 'Oh, come on,' he pleaded, 'this is a big thing for me. It will be the first time I've ever performed in live theatre. Surely you can make an exception?'

The answer was always going to be no. I was sorry in many ways because it would have been good experience for Chris, but I spelled out his position quite plainly. 'You are appearing in Coronation Street and if you want to stay, you do not appear in panto. If I give in to you, everyone will feel free to sign panto contracts. I can't allow that.'

This took place in late spring or early summer and I thought the matter was at an end. Early consideration was, as usual, given to the re-signing of November's annual contracts, and no one was more surprised than me when the casting department told me that Chris Quinten's agent had mentioned in passing that although Chris was delighted to stay with the show, he did have a pantomime obligation to fulfil.

I thought there must have been some mistake, but Chris's agent confirmed the Lincoln booking. I collared Chris and demanded to know what on earth was going on.

His only reply was, 'Well, why not?'

I couldn't believe he hadn't at least had the courtesy to come back to me and spell out why he was signing the pantomime contract against my express wishes.

His excuse was that he was longing to appear on stage. He added flippantly that if there was still an objection he would be happy to sign a new Street contract the moment the Lincoln show finished.

I said it once more. 'Either you get out of the Lincoln contract or you are out of Coronation Street.'

To make it doubly clear, I rang his agent. Chris did his best to wriggle out of the panto deal, but it was legally binding and Equity, the actors' union, would almost certainly have blacklisted any attempt to blow a hole through the agreement.

Sadly, I had to point out that he hadn't broken any Granada contract; simply because he didn't have one. 'You won't be getting one either,' I said. 'I'm writing you out of the show.'

That was my final word, and Chris knew it. I don't think he believed I would ever take the matter so seriously and he went away looking shell-shocked. I had to make an example, if only to drive the point home to Chris or anyone else who believed they could ride roughshod over a perfectly reasonable ruling. Chris Quinten had deliberately defied me, mistakenly believing he was so important to Coronation Street we couldn't afford to lose him.

He wasn't the first to make that mistake, but I had to prove once again that no one but the programme itself is the big star in Coronation Street. Chris's contract was not renewed that November, and it was six months before I decided it was time for forgiveness.

Brian Tilsley was banished to Qatar to team up with his former garage boss servicing trucks in the oil fields. What I kept from Chris while he served out his punishment was that always in the back of my mind was a plan to bring him back. Although he needed to be taught a lesson, he was too good a character to lose.

One day Brian would have to rejoin Gail and the baby, or fall victim to a premature death in the desert sands. It was decided he should play the prodigal dad. The story was discussed at a writers' conference and Harry Kershaw, the Street's former producer who was a very welcome and talented member of the writing team, decided his homecoming should have a sting in its tail. As an added slap for Chris having dared to step out of line, he jokingly suggested Brian should return with a nasty anti-social disease.

Quick to join in, I suggested it should be Tokyo Rose, a very virulent strain which, at that time, had no known cure. The writers roared their approval. That would put an abrupt end to Chris Quinten's lady-killing lifestyle. John Stevenson, quick as a flash, asked whether Tokyo Rose wasn't similar to the affliction rife in the Pennine foothills: Saddleworth Tulip. These lighter moments were always welcome, and took the tension out of story conferences. There was a lot of laughter that day, before we finally talked ourselves out of the whole unsavoury plan, and Brian Tilsley arrived back fragrant and blameless from his Middle East adventures.

20

CORONATION STREET – THIS IS YOUR LIFE

Coronation Street eventually became a happy hunting ground for the team who produce This is Your Life. They made so many sorties into Weatherfield, it would probably be easier to name the major characters who didn't fall victim to Eamonn Andrews's famous red book than those who did.

Every time the Thames Television team swooped, the atmosphere was tension-packed and secretive. The personal stories eventually screened were all dramatically different. But they all shared a staggering degree of behind-the-scenes intrigue, infinitely more exciting than anything the viewers saw as the programme unfolded.

Jack Howarth played Albert Tatlock at his grumpiest when Eamonn confronted him on the Street set. The amiable Irishman was told exactly what he could do with his book, while Jack stomped off to hide in his dressing room until his wife, Betty Murgatroyd, eventually soothed his ruffled feathers and persuaded him to emerge to face a studio packed with old friends.

I helped lead Johnny Briggs so successfully into the trap of a Covent Garden pub, that when Eamonn Andrews was walking towards the cockney actor, Johnny thought the surprise was to be sprung on me.

Bill Waddington, the old soldier Percy Sugden, was more than a little surprised

one afternoon to find his old pal Joe Loss conducting an orchestra in the middle of Euston Station.

'Who told them I was coming?' he quipped. He found the incongruous sight so amusing, he wise-cracked that he was a little disappointed that the two-thousand onlookers hadn't turned up to see him. They had of course. Eamonn Andrews crept up from behind, and tapped him on the shoulder with the time-honoured words.

All the major characters knew they were likely targets for Eamonn's undercover agents. By keeping an ear to the ground I got a fair indication of who would take offence if duped into taking part. Jean Alexander made it quite clear that she would never co-operate under any circumstances, and despite the many requests which the This is Your Life team made, they were wasting their time to think they could uncover the private life of Hilda Ogden. Doris Speed shared Jean's feelings. She fiercely guarded her privacy. The last thing she wanted was the embarrassment of having it paraded before millions. Others went like lambs to the slaughter, and gave me some heart-stopping moments on the way.

The title of This is Your Life was never mentioned at any stage in the planning, and even the subjects were given coded names. But I became so familiar with the

The fearless Percy stops the traffic – just as Bill Waddington halted Euston Station

identities of the show's research and production team, that they only had to mention their names on the telephone to alert me that yet another Coronation Street target had been selected. Their voices became so familiar, I could almost answer the call by asking, 'Who do you have in mind this time?'

'Julie Goodyear,' was once the reply, and another clandestine operation swung into action. The Thames Television team had thoroughly researched her background, but as always they left it to me to lead the unsuspecting star to London. Though I was always devious, I'm surprised no one ever caught on to the fact that whenever I offered an unusual night out in London it was always on a Wednesday. The mid-week factor – the night This is Your Life sprang its surprises, and occasionally transmitted the programme live – should have been the giveaway, but never was.

The 'victim' was always persuaded to skip through Wednesday afternoon's technical run and catch an early afternoon train, so that the rest of the cast could hop aboard the following intercity express. Julie was easily led on the first part of the journey. But even with the best-laid plans, deceptions on the scale we were organising were never without pitfalls.

Julie and I had been guests at a lunch which the international sales division of Granada had hosted for a group of Australian Television executives. I told her that our guests were honouring us with a reciprocal dinner in London and, as we were very keen to win back a slot on the Australian network, I invited her to join this very important promotional operation. Of course, said I, it could eventually mean a trip to Australia.

Julie happily agreed. She had recently returned from holiday where she had met the latest love in her life and, as they were shortly to announce their engagement, she wondered whether he could come too. I checked with Thames TV and they instantly made the young man their number one guest. Little did they suspect the invitation would bring about a near disaster.

I so stressed the importance of the dinner that I could hardly refuse Julie's request for yet another addition to our party. Knowing we would be pushed for time at the London end, and wanting very much to impress our Australian friends, she suggested her favourite make-up lady should come along too. At this stage I thought the whole operation was getting a little out of hand, but didn't dare rock the boat. Thames were telephoned again, and yet another person was sworn to secrecy.

The arrangements gave all four of us first-class seats in the first carriage of the London train. The driver would be given a precise mark on the Euston platform at which to bring his engine to a halt, and there at the carriage steps would be a red carpet and a brass band to welcome a

hopefully stunned-looking Julie with the tune of 'She's a lassie from Lancashire'.

So detailed were the preparations that whenever Julie went off to powder her nose, I was to creep around the carriage explaining to some no doubt perplexed fellow passengers that Julie must be allowed off the train first, and that the reason would become perfectly clear once we reached London. To make sure that passengers from other carriages didn't come through to make a quick exit at Euston, the guard was to lock the connecting door.

The plan might have worked like a charm had the leading carriage not been a non-smoker. Julie wasn't prepared to travel anywhere without a cigarette and the only option was to move down the train.

Swift rearrangements for the door-locking operation were made with the guard who, from thereon, gave me great knowing winks of satisfaction every time he passed. How Julie didn't notice I'll never know. As the journey progressed I managed to pass my mysterious message to all aboard and, nearing London, the only passengers unaware that something unexpected awaited at our destination were a young couple who boarded at Watford.

Luckily they were sitting behind us, and I made an excuse to get up and whisper, 'For reasons which will become clear later, will you please not get off the train before the fair-haired lady I'm travelling with.'

'It's all right,' they replied. 'We're from Thames Television.'

The couple had a radio link with Euston to warn of the moment of our approach, and exactly where we were sitting. But luck wasn't with us and in some last-minute confusion, the train driver halted at the wrong spot, leaving us to alight some twenty yards from the red carpet. Passengers scurried past, while Julie puzzled why a band was playing a familiar north-country melody.

I was never sure whether Julie had at some stage put two and two together and rumbled our plans. If she was expecting Eamonn to step from the crowd, she gave an Oscar-winning performance of mock surprise. The star reception and unexpected adulation were Julie's idea of heaven, and she was whisked off, beaming with pleasure, to the Thames studios where a large audience was waiting to hear her remarkable life story.

Unfortunately they had a long wait. Julie may have been smiling from ear to ear, but the gods were not. The train carrying Bet Lynch's Coronation Street pals was delayed for an hour after fire broke out in a kitchen car. It threw the studio schedule into chaos and the delay would have been even greater had the ladies of our cast not agreed to save precious time by commandeering one of the train's toilets in which to change into their evening gowns and brush up their make-up. The show was finally recorded, for transmission two weeks later. As a cavalcade of family, stars and friends was introduced by Eamonn, Julie spent the entire half-hour lovingly gripping the hand of the handsome new man in her life. The following Wednesday morning I heard a snippet of gossip which threw everything into a panic. Not only had Julie stormed through a major fall-out with her fiancé and thrown him out of her home, but a blow-by-blow account of the sensational bust-up was destined for the headlines of a Sunday newspaper.

It would be published three days before Julie's This is Your Life was scheduled for transmission. The least I

could do was to alert Thames that the boyfriend who starred so prominently in the programme was now out on his ear. To save everyone embarrassment, I suggested the only way the Julie Goodyear show could be rescued was to transmit it that very night. At first Thames said it would be impossible because that evening's programme, on football manager Laurie McMenemy, was scheduled to go out live. I spoke to the producer, Jack Crawshaw, who was putting the final touches to his detailed planning at Southampton's football ground.

'Julie has kicked him out,' I explained. 'The love affair is over and the whole of Britain will know of the break-up by this weekend.'

Jack sounded stunned. 'Stay at the end of your 'phone,' he said. 'I'll call you back.'

He must have taken a lonely walk around the pitch to gather his thoughts, then telephoned to say the McMenemy story would be held over, and Julie's programme transmitted in its place.

It was a successful face-saving operation. Eamonn later sent me a note which read: 'I don't know whether to thank you more for everything you did before, during or after the show.'

Some time later, Thames came on again to say the team had targeted Roy Barraclough, Julie's screen husband, Alec Gilroy. This time I deeply suspected I would get no thanks from anyone. Roy hadn't been with the Street long enough for me to have gathered the slightest hint as to whether he would be happy about taking part in the programme. But when I thought of Roy's wonderfully colourful stage career, I began to convince myself that perhaps, after all, he would go along with the surprise. The way we finally agreed to close the net, however, made me seriously nervous.

Something must have gone badly wrong with Thames schedules, for instead of giving me two or three months' warning of the subject, they gave me less than two weeks. They said that most of the background research was complete, and it was simply a matter of how and when we could spring the trap. I knew Roy had a two-week break coming up, and vaguely recalled he had said something about teaming up with Tom Elliot, a good friend and one of our story-line associates, for a holiday in Spain. Tom confirmed they were booked to fly to Torremolinos on the Sunday before the Wednesday earmarked for This is Your Life.

I went back on to Thames to discuss the problem, and they offered to meet all the expenses of flying him home for twenty-four hours if only I could think of a good enough excuse to break into his holiday. Once again, when the game reached match point, the ball was squarely in my court.

I then realised Roy had five very important scenes to record in the Rovers last thing on the Friday afternoon before his departure. I began to piece together a plot to pretend that, due to human error, those scenes had been lost. Time would never allow us to wait until his return from holiday before remaking them.

Thames thought it a wonderful idea. I'm afraid I didn't altogether share their enthusiasm, but it was simply a matter of whether I had the courage to lie my way through it.

The suspicion nagged at me that I could scupper a friendship just by interrupting Roy's well-deserved rest in the sunshine. If it turned out that he didn't like the idea of appearing in This is Your Life I knew I would be in even deeper trouble. My apprehensions were shouting loudly for a cancellation of the plot; Thames TV and Roy's agent were persuading me that he would be delighted. I finally agreed to go ahead with my part of the bargain when I was told that Roy's elderly parents would be deeply disappointed if the show was called off.

I proposed to wait until Saturday before telling Roy that his scenes had been mysteriously and disastrously wiped from the video, and asking if he would be prepared to come back from Spain to make a new recording. When the moment came I was so nervous I kept walking to the 'phone, then not daring to pick it up. I had rehearsed a complicated pack of lies and although I half-contented my conscience that they were all white ones, I knew that if I wasn't very careful, I would never carry it off.

Finally I poured a stiff drink and dialled. It rang out, an unanswered anti-climax. Not knowing where to find Roy, I called Tom Elliot, and asked him to relay a message that there had been a disaster at the studio, and that I would be waiting at home for his call.

Finally Roy telephoned and in a voice measured to whip up sympathy, I began: 'Listen and swallow hard, because you are going to find this difficult to believe. I've had a message from the studio to say something has gone very wrong, and the last five scenes of Friday's recording have been wiped clean.' I assured Roy that when the details emerged somebody's head would roll.

'I should bloody think so, too,' he replied feelingly. 'But what are you going to do about it?' I must have taken a very deep breath. The hook was baited. Would the fish take it? 'At this moment I'm talking off the top of my head, because I don't even know when I can book studio space,' I began. 'But if another recording can be slotted in one day next week, would you be prepared to fly home?'

In truth, I knew exactly when he would have to come back, but it was so soon after his scheduled arrival in Spain, I didn't dare tell him.

There seemed to be a long silence at the other end before Roy replied. 'Well listen, Bill, those are important scenes and the show has to go on. It's a bit of a tall order, but I'll just have to come back.'

This was no time to lose my nerve but I have to admit I was sorely tempted to confess all and call the whole thing off. As I put down the telephone I had no doubt that shortly I was going to have to face one very angry actor.

Tom, his wife, and Roy flew off the following day, but as luck would have it their flight was delayed and they didn't arrive at the resort until the early hours of Monday morning. Roy would barely have had time to unpack his bags before I 'phoned his hotel to break the news that the only studio space I could find at such short notice had been booked for first thing on Wednesday morning. The truth was that This is Your Life had reserved a studio for a Tuesday evening recording.

'But I've only just bloody well got here,' the actor complained.

I launched into an explanation of the complicated travel arrangements for Tuesday afternoon. He was to fly from Malaga to Heathrow where, in case there were delays and he missed the shuttle connection, a private executive jet would be standing by to fly him on to Manchester where a chauffeur-driven car would be waiting. He was far from happy, but agreed to meet what he obviously regarded as his professional responsibility to Coronation Street.

From thereon, Eamonn's team took over. Eamonn's own chauffeur collected Roy at the airport and, saying he knew of a shortcut to avoid snarled-up motorway traffic, he dived down a country road.

There they came across Julie Goodyear's Rolls Royce broken down with what looked like an AA man delving under its bonnet. To find his co-star marooned in the Cheshire countryside was quite a surprise for Roy. But when a beaming AA man turned and said, 'Roy Barraclough, This is Your Life,' the actor almost exploded.

'Oh no it bloody well isn't,' Roy stormed. The ensuing verbal barrage succeeded in wiping the seemingly permanent smile from Eamonn's face. There very nearly wasn't a show. Roy was absolutely livid. I had expected trouble and Roy's agent had promised to be there in case he was needed to cool the actor down. It wasn't enough. Some very angry accusations were hurled about that country lane before Roy could be persuaded to continue his journey. On the way, Julie and Eamonn went through every argument they could think of to coax him into doing the show and many more heated words were exchanged before his fury finally began to subside. He only agreed when they told him his mum and dad were excitedly awaiting their big moment.

Throughout the recording Roy was outrageous. He threw me a filthy look as I came on, and when Dora Bryan emerged from behind the curtain, Roy was overheard to say, 'I don't even know her.' Heavy editing had to be done before the show was transmitted, and at a reception later, Roy told me quite seriously, 'I never want to speak to you again. Dragging me all the way from Spain . . . well that's it.'

He was in no mood for fence-mending; furious about the deception, and quite unwilling to accept my apologies. I contented myself with the thought that time cures all ills, and hoped I would be forgiven by the time his holiday was over. Thankfully I was right. Tom Elliot took most of the stick. Roy rightly assumed he must have been party to the plot and pinned a 'do not disturb' note to his hotel-room door which stayed there for several days, until the sunshine and sangria massaged Roy's anger into some measure of forgiveness.

Bill with Jean – she has now left the series, but not before making Hilda Ogden into a legend

21

HILDA LEAVES
THE COLDEST PLACE ON EARTH

Even in those dark days, before central heating, Scott of the Antarctic might just have been exaggerating when he said there was no place on earth quite so cold as an English bedroom. Jean Alexander, for one, would have taken him to task. Nowhere, she swore, after many a winter Monday morning on the original outdoor set of Coronation Street, could match the maliciously bone-numbing chill of that wretched spot.

I suspect she was right. I haven't yet met anyone in the cast or production crew who would disagree with her. The set was built, dank and sunless, in the shadow of a dripping railway viaduct and Jean hated it.

In the earliest days of the programme, the frontage of the terrace was but flimsy scenery, constructed in whatever space the indoor studios would allow. Pavement and roadway were painted on the floor, and the set was contained within measurements so small that the writers had to take care that no one episode included houses at both ends. All the scenes had to be set either alongside the Rovers Return, or at the end with the corner shop. It was impossible to fit the whole street in.

This greatly restricted any suggestion of what might have passed as open-air filming but when Richard Everitt, the producer of the day, discovered the real-life replica of Tommy Deakin's archway,

only a stone's throw away from Granada's headquarters, Coronation Street headed for the great outdoors. The little plot of land around the arch was leased from the railway authority, and carpenters built a life-like replica in the forlorn hope that their wood and canvas construction would stand up to the elements. It didn't, of course, so, within severe constrictions of both budget and space, the façade of Coronation Street was rebuilt in brick.

This was the set which I inherited; one just good enough to fool most of the people all of the time. For the cast and crew it was a rough-and-ready affair, never warm, even on the sunniest of days and pure Siberian savagery in the winter months.

The only building with a fully slated and reasonably weatherproof roof was the Community Centre. Even so it was extremely primitive and on Monday mornings, Gordon McKellar, the production manager, would courageously turn out early to clear up the abuse and filth of the weekend vandals. American actors and actresses would never have tolerated the conditions. I can't begin to describe some of the appalling scenes which greeted Gordon.

The set was surrounded by high walls and guarded by two great gates topped with what appeared to be impenetrable barbed wire. But that was no protection

'The coldest place on earth' – the original outdoor set, as dismal as it looks. The gap is where Len built his new house.

against the vandals, or in fact members of the public innocently wanting to take a peek into Coronation Street. The more intrepid climbed on the roofs of their cars to scale the walls, while others found their way into the neighbouring railway goods yard and risked being hit by trains to stare down from the viaduct.

I have no doubt many of those sightseers expected to discover the stars of their favourite programme living there permanently, and probably thought we just came along with our cameras on Mondays and Wednesdays to catch up on the everyday story of their lives. A lot of folk must have put themselves in danger and gone to a great deal of physical effort only to discover the disappointing truth. At one point, there was so much concern that someone would be injured, or even killed, falling from the wall or viaduct, that a viewing-hatch was cut into the gates.

The whole set was a cheerless place, but come hail, rain, or the sun which never shone there, this was where the week always started and the outside street-scenes were filmed. In the depths of winter those mornings were horrendous. The houses were nothing but façades, with windows and a front door. There was half a roof to complete the illusion, but a peep behind the scenery revealed only supporting trusses, and an area open to all weathers.

It really was Jean Alexander's idea of hell, and I had every sympathy for her and the rest of the cast who so stoically braved it. So often a character such as Hilda would be called on to wait behind the front door of her supposedly cosy little home, when in fact she was standing with her teeth chattering and a freezing wind tugging at her skirt. Annie Walker complained her mouth was often so frozen, she had the greatest difficulty speaking her lines.

It was always at these moments that a camera would give trouble, or some such technical hitch would delay filming. Everyone would be so busy trying to sort out the difficulty that members of the cast would be left standing behind their doors ignorant of the hold-up and waiting impatiently for their cue to step into the street.

The set had to be made a mite more comfortable, and one improvement I engineered was to erect a six-foot wall a few feet behind each front door, and have it roofed over. In effect, a tiny hallway was created, complete with staircase in case the camera glimpsed inside. Most important, portable heaters could be installed in the worst weather, to give some warmth.

It was often so cold that heaters were set up on the pavements just out of camera shot. The cast had a makeshift headquarters in the Community Centre, but its leaking roof and visiting vandals made it an almost intolerable shelter. Gordon McKellar, finally tiring of his attempts to keep the place habitable, suggested a caravan should be towed on and off the site as required. That was infinitely more comfortable, but it was only for the principal artists. The extras still had to fend for themselves.

Space was at a premium every way we turned. The site was incredibly small and it would have been impossible to fit in full-scale replicas of the six house frontages we needed, plus the Rovers and Alf's shop at either end. The problem was solved by scaling the whole thing down. Each house was no more than six feet wide and a mini car would overlap on either side of a frontage. It certainly proved that the camera does lie, and very few people noticed its Lilliputian proportions.

We only gave the game away when there was a dramatic fire in the building which is now Baldwin's factory. The fire engine dwarfed everything, and observant viewers spotted the miniature scale of the street.

If Coronation Street hadn't become a national monument it would probably have been knocked down years ago under one of the slum clearance orders which flattened the surrounding areas. But it was spared the bulldozers until Granada's own planners decided it should be resited much closer to the main studio. This finally came about with the creation of Granada Tours, an adventurous plan to open the company's major outdoor sets to the public. For the first time fans could actually take a stroll along Coronation Street and call in for a pint at a replica of the Rovers.

The original set was sited to take advantage of an authentic railway viaduct. After the rebuilding, only the railway arch was a total sham. The street itself was lovingly recreated in reclaimed Salford brick. The cobblestones ran in the right direction and there was even enough space to build a new house. Number seven had been missing since its demolition in a gas explosion years before. As we prepared to move to our new site, Len Fairclough set about the rebuilding work to provide a new home

First day filming on the new outdoor set

for himself and Rita.

It also gave us the opportunity to solve the longstanding mystery of the missing Rovers Return gents' loo. Keen-eyed viewers had noticed that in the geography of the old street, any man visiting the pub's toilet would have to open a door leading directly into Albert Tatlock's kitchen. They were right of course. There was no space for the toilet. I jokingly made excuses to those who spotted the error that it was the prime cause of old Albert's grumpiness. However, the new dimensions were generous enough to allow a little entry to run between the Rovers' wall and the Tatlock household; just enough space to relieve our embarrassment.

The houses were still empty shells, but now they did keep out the weather. Surrounding buildings didn't hide the sunshine either, and that lifted everyone's spirits. Hilda Ogden threw away her thermal underwear, and wore a genuine smile on Monday mornings.

Despite the hardships Hilda endured, thousands of Mrs Mops would dearly have loved to change headscarves with her, and hundreds wrote offering to stand in if ever she wanted a break. Those generous offers had always to be politely refused, but I was delighted to make sure at least one cleaning lady was given the red-carpet treatment down at the Rovers.

One morning after a party at Herriots,

a night spot along the road from the studios, I discovered to my horror that my wallet containing eighty pounds and all my credit cards was missing. A telephone call to the club ended my anxiety. The wallet had been found by a cleaner and was in the club safe.

The manager insisted he had his own policy of rewarding staff for deeds of honesty, and would not hear of a contribution from me. But when I opened the wallet, a little note gave me the perfect opportunity.

It read: 'Dear Mr Podmore, I realise who you are. If Hilda Ogden ever leaves or goes off sick, I'll be very happy to stand in for her.'

We made that Mrs Mop very happy indeed. Jean and I sent her an invitation to visit the studios and, dusters in hand, she and Hilda stood proudly side-by-side while the press lined up for a photo session.

Hilda Ogden was a legend. Universities wanted to make her their rector; a Welsh rugby team hailed her as their mascot; even the Falklands Fleet urgently called for a picture of their pin-up complete with curlers, to inspire the troops for battle. Legends live for ever, but I knew that the self-effacing, quiet, auburn-haired lady who lived in a rather posh Southport semi would one day close the door on number 13 Coronation Street for the last time.

I will never forget the day she told me it was about to happen. The loss of any character, particularly a major one, always left me feeling that a chunk of the Street had been torn away. I knew by now it could survive great losses; nevertheless, the disappearance of Hilda Ogden was a daunting prospect. I really did think Hilda's retirement would be one of the great watersheds, and I was dreading the inevitable moment.

When my secretary put her head round the door one May morning to say Jean would like a chat, some sixth sense told me the news would be bad. My worst fears were confirmed by the fact that Jean closed the door behind her.

'Are you sitting comfortably?' she asked, knowing that what she was about to tell me was the last thing I wanted to hear.

'Not as comfortable as I would like,' I replied. 'I think I can guess what you have come to tell me.'

Jean tried her best to break the news gently.

'If that is what you are thinking, then you are right,' she confirmed. 'I'm afraid I shall not be signing a new contract. I feel it's time to leave.'

My heart sank. The dreaded moment had arrived. I knew an appeal was hopeless, but I tried anyway.

'I don't suppose there is anything I can say or do to make you change your mind?'

'I'm afraid not, Bill,' she replied. 'I haven't arrived at this conclusion overnight. I've been thinking about it for a long time. In fact, I gave the question very serious thought last year. Before I retire altogether, I would like to play some different roles.'

That is exactly what she did and has thoroughly enjoyed herself. For public consumption, Jean announced she was heartily sick of standing on draughty railway stations week in, week out, waiting for trains which were rarely on time and sometimes didn't turn up at all. Every rail commuter will sympathise, although I suspect it was only one of the reasons she decided she'd had enough of Hilda and needed to stretch her formidable talents on some other stage.

Jean Alexander chose to travel by train, although there was an allowance available had she wished to cut out the daily journey and spend weekdays in a Manchester hotel. More often than not, she walked to and from the station and when, after she hung up her pinafore for the last time, she announced how thankful she was to put the travelling behind her, I received a postbag of angry letters demanding to know how I had dared treat such a great star so disgracefully. Why had I not laid on a limousine? The answer was simple. The Dynasty life is not Jean Alexander's style and never will be. I shouldered most of the blame, as far as the public were concerned, for allowing her to spend such weary hours travelling. But the actress once voted the most popular woman in Britain after the Queen, the Queen Mother and Princess Diana, chose to keep the lowest profile possible.

Jean never married and, apart from acting, the great loves of her life were her home, her garden, classical music and cats. When she shook out Hilda's curlers for the last time in December 1987, her close friend, Betty Driver, was asked to suggest a suitable farewell present. A flight of ducks or a new 'muriel' might have been appropriate, but Betty had the perfect gift in mind. For many years, Jean had longed to own a particular ornamental cat exquisitely crafted in fine French crystal, but had never plucked up the courage to spend what must have seemed an outrageous sum of money on something purely decorative. Jean was thrilled. The cat was as tastefully beautiful as her famous pot ducks were naff.

One other treasure Jean richly deserved takes pride of place beside the cat in her home. It is the award she won from the Royal Television Society – TV's equivalent of an Oscar – for her poignantly memorable performance when she finally set free all the grief Hilda had

so bravely bottled up after the death of her beloved Stan. It was presented for the 'Best Television Performance of the Year', the first time such an accolade had been bestowed on a soap star. To my mind, it was a recognition long overdue.

Coronation Street's scriptwriting team, with Jean's total approval, had decided that Hilda would never allow herself to shed a tear in public no matter how great her sadness. We all thought long and hard about how she might deal with her husband's death. The breakdown had to come some time, and we chose the moment when Hilda unwrapped the sad little parcel she brought home from the hospital, which contained Stan's few personal effects. Jean's playing of that scene was devastating; as she closed Stan's spectacle case the nation wept with her.

The Royal Television Society award belonged to Jean, but, true to her nature, she generously shared it with Bernard Youens and reminded the audience of his contribution to their twenty-year partnership.

It was a great comic partnership, and they were firm friends, yet their friendship rarely extended past Granada's doors. They played Scrabble together non-stop, while waiting for studio calls, but visited each other's homes only a couple of times in all the years they embodied one of television's most famous and enduring marriages.

Bernard's death was a tragic blow and, during his last years, I shouldered harsh criticism for allowing him to battle on against obviously failing health. In his youth Bernard was a handsome leading actor, an Errol Flynn character, who joined Granada as a station announcer. Acting is always a precarious profession and Bernard had endured the lean times. He had even turned his hand a couple of

Hilda mourns

Hilda and Stan – an unforgettable partnership

times to being a pub landlord, but ended up deeply in debt. Coronation Street offered him an audition during the original casting, and only the security of his announcer's role stopped him throwing caution to the winds and taking another foray into acting. I like to think it was a good decision. He might have been offered a less durable role, and we would have been denied our colossally lovable champion for the nation's layabouts.

Bernard suffered his first stroke before I took over as producer. The attack damaged the muscles in his face, and for a while he worked with a speech thera-

pist in an effort to regain their use. A second stroke left him with an even greater speech difficulty. His words often sounded slurred and the condition became more and more pronounced. Eventually, when he found it almost impossible to handle complete sentences, the scripts were written so Hilda did most of the talking. Stan was expected to respond with just a word or two, or more effectively, one of his endearing grunts and a long-suffering expression.

Some accused me of cruelty, allowing him to suffer such indignity. I would have agreed wholeheartedly, had Bernard ever expressed the slightest wish to pack it in. For me or anyone else in the show even to suggest it would have been unforgivable. He wanted nothing more than to stay with the programme until the very last moment, and once confided in me that his dearest wish was actually to die sitting in his chair on the set. I understood exactly how he felt. Whenever I enquired how he was, he went to some lengths to make it clear that he could still handle the job. As long as he could stand, Bernard wanted to stay. Sometimes even that was difficult, for he suffered from arthritis, but the Coronation Street cast and crew were always glad to give him all the support he needed.

Helen Worth, who plays Gail Tilsley. Television does occasionally mirror real life: both Brian and Chris married vivacious blondes! (Photo: Bill Podmore)

22

OUR ROMEO
MEETS HIS MATCH

One of the many little Coronation Street myths which have gone unchallenged over the years revolves around who actually made the telephone call which finally put the brakes on the free-wheeling love life of Chris Quinten.

Helen Worth, who plays his screen wife, was originally awarded full credit for picking up a hotel 'phone to trigger off the romantic chain of events which led Chris to the altar and made Gail Tilsley a widow. In fact it was me.

Helen was certainly there, and eagerly joined in the plot. But when I put that fateful call through to Chris's room, neither of us suspected for a moment that it would change all our lives.

New Zealand Television actually invented the charity telethon, and Street stars were always high on its invitation list to these events. At that time, late summer 1988, they were a few months behind our viewers, and were watching the remarriage of Gail and Brian after her affair with Ian Latimer.

Brian and Gail were big news, and the natural first choice for the telethon people. Helen invited along her long-time boy-friend, Michael Angelis, who played Chrissie in the award-winning Boys from the Blackstuff. The three of us flew into Auckland on the same day, and Chris joined us the following morning after stopping off in Australia to make a personal appearance at a charity motor-racing event.

Our hosts had laid on a traditional Maori welcome and we had arranged to meet in our hotel foyer. Chris was late. Helen, Michael and I were sitting on a sofa when two very elegant and attractive ladies walked in. I guessed they were mother and daughter, but they were so striking I wondered who they were.

The mother sat on the settee opposite and said good morning in a southern American drawl. Her daughter, a beautiful, tall blonde, went off to use the 'phone.

I nudged Helen: 'I can't wait for Chris to clock this one.'

She was obviously thinking exactly the same and replied, 'Neither can I.'

I went to the house 'phones to remind Chris he was late.

'Down in a minute, down in a minute,' he spluttered, and sure enough, minutes later he came bounding down the stairs. He was just about to say Hi, when he spotted the girl on the 'phone. It literally stopped him in his tracks.

'Who's that, who's that?' he kept repeating.

We all roared with laughter and exclaimed, 'Exactly as predicted, Chris.'

Chris and I were booked to take part in the telethon from Christchurch, because we wanted to go ski-ing later. I said to Helen that if that young lady was heading there too, Chris was going to

Chris Quinten living it up in New Zealand (Photo: Bill Podmore)

find it very distracting. She was, and he did.

She was Leeza Gibbons, American TV star and co-host of a coast-to-coast networked chat show, with fans by the million and a salary to match. She had to make a quick overnight trip back to Sydney so Chris and I flew down to Christchurch with her mum, Jean.

We all met up again later at a getting-to-know-you buffet for the telethon stars. Afterwards, when Jean had gone off to bed, Chris suggested Leeza and I should have a nightcap in his room. Leeza perched on the end of the bed and I settled on a sofa while Chris fixed the drinks. I'd hardly taken a sip before I distinctly felt I might be in the way, and opted for a tactful retreat.

The next morning I was woken by a 'phone call from Chris, bubbling over with excitement. 'Guess what, Bill? I'm in love.'

'Don't you mean lust?' I replied cynically.

'No, no, this is the real thing. This is it. She's wonderful.'

'Hang on,' I said. 'I'll be along to throw a bucket of cold water over you.'

Chris and Leeza threw themselves into the telethon and didn't take a break for the whole twenty-four hours. Chris's energy was unbounded. Few could seriously hope to keep up with him once he gets going. He's an ex-Second Generation dancer, and whether it was all sparked off by his new-found love I don't know, but he did back-flips on stage and joined strict routine dance groups as if he spent his life rehearsing with them.

Mum Jean was more than a little impressed, too. We went back to the hotel for a rest and a meal, and she asked me whether Chris had any serious girlfriends back home. I said there had been more than a few over the years but as I far as I knew there was no one currently enjoying his particular affection.

She asked how he had come to join Coronation Street. I explained it had happened some time ago, when I was searching for a young actor to play the son of an established character. I had arranged to audition young hopefuls in London, and Chris was first to appear. He walked in with such an engaging grin I instantly liked him. We had a long chat, and although he had little or no acting experience, he had a charisma I knew our younger fans would love. I decided to take a gamble, and told Chris bluntly that he would have to learn his acting skills along the way. In the early days it presented him with problem after problem, but his personality carried him through, and finally he slotted into the show.

He gave us our fair share of headaches on and off the set, but some magic moments, too. To this day, Helen Worth still giggles, and wonders how she managed to act out the bedroom scene which mended their battered marriage after the Ian Latimer affair. It was billed as the sexiest scene in the history of British soap and the press had a field day. For late-night Channel 4 it would, they claimed, have been powerful stuff, but the thought of Gail and Brian having a roll in the sack in Coronation Street was simply shocking.

It all guaranteed millions glued to their sets, the audience ratings rocketed, and

in a rather raunchy grapple, our own little macho-man, Brian, finally won his chance to bare his broad chest and prove his manhood.

That's what the viewers saw. It was Coronation Street's first sexy bedroom scene in its twenty-odd-year history, and Chris managed to reduce the first take to the level of a Whitehall farce. Helen was waiting in bed, respectably covered in her Marks & Spencer's nightie and looking fairly nervous, when Chris made his entrance. He stopped at the foot of the bed and threw open his dressing gown like some demented subway flasher.

He was sporting the hugest pair of blue cotton underpants anyone had ever seen. Quite where the wardrobe department had found them is anyone's guess. But they came up to his armpits and the sight of him standing there reduced the whole set to tears of laughter.

Once the telethon was over Leeza and her mum were heading off to Queenstown, Helen and Michael were staying in Dunedin, and Chris and I had booked to go ski-ing in the mountains fifty miles from Christchurch across the Canterbury Plains. Chris 'phoned me again from his room and announced, 'Let's have a champagne breakfast to celebrate.'

'Celebrate what?' I asked.

'To celebrate the fact that I'm in love.'

The Dom Perignon was wonderful but it did nothing for my ski-ing.

One minor irritation of the New Zealand trip was the mislaying of Chris's suitcase en route from Auckland. Our hosts whisked him into Christchurch to buy a complete new wardrobe which eventually, in a moment of typical Quinten madness, I was to inherit.

We flew back from the ski-ing to find Helen, Michael and the missing bag waiting at the hotel. We swapped stories – mainly about Chris's new love – and planned a second ski-ing trip for the morning. Chris never joined us. He was on the telephone before breakfast rather plaintively asking, 'You won't be cross, will you?'

'Why, what have you done?'

'It's more what I want to do,' he explained. 'You see, I've arranged a flight to Queenstown to be with Leeza.'

'This is getting very serious, Chris,' I cautioned.

'I know, I know,' he replied. 'But you won't mind if I go, will you?'

'Chris, I don't mind what you do just so long as you are back in Manchester for rehearsals on the day you are supposed to be there.'

'I'll be there,' he promised. 'Even better, I'll meet you all in Honolulu on Thursday.'

We met briefly at breakfast, where Chris apologised he hadn't room to pack the new wardrobe the TV folk had provided, and as we took the same sizes, I was to take anything I fancied.

His room looked as though a bomb had gone off. There were clothes everywhere, T-shirts, sweaters, slacks, all brand new with the labels still attached. The one item I'm sure he didn't mean to leave behind lay on the bedside table. It was a lovely photograph of Leeza.

I thought to myself, this boy is really smitten.

The thought was still with me when we got to Honolulu. Chris was supposed to arrive the day after us, but by mid-afternoon there was no sign of the love-struck lad. Leeza was due back home in Los Angeles, and I half expected Chris might have jetted off with her.

I needn't have worried. I was settled at the poolside when I was distracted by Hawaiian music from the hotel courtyard. It was suggested I should take a look.

A group of giggling island girls were doing a grass-skirted hula-hula dance with Chris Quinten in the middle, hips swaying in perfect time, and grinning from ear to ear.

23

OUR ROMEO
MEETS HIS END

Chris Quinten was born lucky. New Zealand Television carried him half-way around the world at their expense to meet the great new love in his life, and British Airways picked up the tab a few weeks later when Chris flew out from Britain to see her again.

From Honolulu we all flew to LA, where, due to some computer gremlin, or more likely overbooking, there was a ticket mix-up and only two seats remained unclaimed in the first-class cabin for the flight to London. Actually there were three, but staff at the check-in desk explained they were expecting a late-arrival passenger described only as a VIP.

Chris couldn't let that pass. 'What do you mean?' he said, pointing at me. 'This man is a VIP.' Higher authority was quickly called, and I was awarded the third seat. This just left the question of where Chris would sit, and the airline unwittingly offered the perfect solution. They said if he would accept downgrading to super-club class, the airline would present him with a free return ticket from Heathrow to LA for a date of his choice.

Chris snatched their hands off at that. He had a scheduled two-week break from the programme coming up, and proposed to spend it with Leeza. I thought two weeks' solid contact would sort the relationship out one way or the other. It certainly did, and Chris came

home to announce they were planning a December wedding.

His feet still hadn't touched the ground. Apart from Leeza, he had fallen in love with the LA lifestyle. But Manchester in November is a long way from the Californian sunshine and Chris Quinten came back to the cold grey light of Quay Street, with a major problem on his mind.

Obviously Leeza was not in a position to pack up her lucrative career to chance her arm in Britain where the pay scales are dramatically different. I don't think Chris considered this a remote possibility for one second.

But he had his own career to consider and when he came to me I don't think he had really made up his mind what he wanted to do. Ideally he didn't want to close the Coronation Street door completely. But he knew that marriage meant his immediate future lay across the Atlantic; in Tinsel Town, where every waiter is an actor out of work.

I felt he hoped to get a new career going, but he needed to be able to regard the Street as a bolt hole to run to if things didn't work out. The psychology was wrong from the start. But, although I didn't entirely agree with his thinking, we were great friends and I promised the character of Brian Tilsley would not be killed off.

It was a promise I was soon to regret.

Sadly I couldn't make it to Chris's wedding. The date clashed with Coronation Street's twenty-eighth anniversary party, an important milestone in itself, but a particularly important evening for me. It was to be my last Street Christmas party as producer, for retirement was only weeks away.

While Chris was in Los Angeles making the final arrangements I called a story-line conference to write Brian out. I had some ideas and needed to flesh out the bones. There had been a girlfriend in Brian Tilsley's life in the last days of his split from Gail during the Ian Latimer affair. He could go off with her after yet another bust-up with Gail. It could after all be argued that Gail had always been reluctant to remarry Brian. She had expressed deep misgivings about it on more than one occasion, and really only agreed to get back together for the sake of their children.

When it came down to the nitty gritty at the story conference, however, this idea was weak and full of holes. It had all happened before; and if Chris Quinten ever did return, just where would he slot back into the Street? The garage would presumably be long gone. There seemed little point in bringing him back just to live with his mum.

Whichever way we assembled the pieces the jigsaw wouldn't fit, and after a lot of soul-searching and heartache we came to the inevitable conclusion that Brian would have to die. The Street's nine regular writers were around that table and there wasn't a dissenting voice. Once the decision had been reached we designed a story that whatever relationship he had with Gail had irretrievably broken down; Brian was going out to discos to put a bit of fun back into his life and hopefully to meet the odd girlfriend. He would try to protect a young lady from a bunch of thugs outside a night club, and be stabbed in the attack which followed. Sad as it was, at least Brian would be dying a hero.

I knew, however, that would be little compensation to Chris when he heard. In fact I knew he would be terribly upset that I had changed my mind and agreed to kill his character off.

Someone said, 'I wouldn't tell him if I were you. He might not come back at all.' At the time I thought that was good advice and decided to keep it under wraps. For the first time ever the story-line was not distributed to the various Granada departments; our cloak-and-dagger plans were confined to our tight little group.

But the Granada moles were already digging: either that or the Manchester press has a finely-developed sixth sense tuned to pluck our ideas out of the ether. Within a matter of days the story-line was leaked.

Chris actually read about it in Los Angeles but dismissed it as misplaced guesswork, or the usual tabloid mischief. He arrived back in Britain full of beans, brimming over with tales of Los Angeles life and proudly clutching a bundle of photos of his new million-dollar home in the Hollywood hills.

The euphoria ended the instant he was handed the script. Naturally he was desperately upset about being killed off and wanted to jump on the next plane home. I think he would have done if Helen hadn't sat him down and laid it on the line that if he backed out, Equity, the actors' union, might black him in Britain.

It didn't help that I was away on a skiing trip the week he arrived back in Manchester, and had no opportunity to explain until six days later. Chris con-

Brian's death

fronted me with his anger and disappointment; all of it deserved. He laid into me. 'I thought we were such great friends that you of all people could have told me of the decision while I was in LA. Did you really think I wouldn't come back? I'm amazed you didn't trust me.'

I could only apologise, tell him I was desperately sorry and plead, 'Don't make me feel any worse because I'm already feeling awful about it.' I explained the reasoning I had gone through with the writers and had to spell out that even if we had kept our promise to hold the door open and kept Brian alive, it didn't necessarily mean we would ever have invited him to walk through it.

We chatted for a long time. In the end I told him he was a young man going to the new world with a new wife. The last thing he wanted if he was to create a new career in America was the thought in the back of his mind that if all else failed, he could pick up the pieces in Coronation Street. That was not the incentive he needed to push himself to the top. He finally adm''' made some kind of sens^ ^well champagne he had wn

Granada had killed him off in revenge for the less savoury headlines he had generated in his Coronation Street career. This was nonsense.

Once Chris had gained his confidence in the programme he enjoyed his fame. He loved discos and the attention of pretty girls, and had the energy for it. He revelled in the club scene. This was all very healthy, but then he was persuaded to join a Manchester nightclub venture and brought his world crashing around his ears.

It left him bankrupt and £60,000 in debt. But instead of going down, as many might have done under that kind of pressure, Chris spent the next twelve months scorching around Britain making any personal appearance he could, and paid off his creditors. Those who believe the woodentop image that newspapers loved to paint badly misjudge him. Chris Quinten is a very shrewd young man who knows what he wants and just how to get it.

I admired his vitality, physical fitness and dedication to staying in shape. Occasionally I had to rein that energy in, but whatever the incident, the truth was always burred by newspaper headlines. Often Chris would beat me to it, arriving in the office before the newspapers reached my desk to explain the true facts.

He couldn't move without the tabloids making something out of nothing. There may have been incidents when he deserved his share of blame, but by the ne the news reached my ears, the press d blown everything out of proportion. he end, Chris refused to make per- l appearances, fearing what stunt ress would pull next. He had his e in the end. His patience finally d; he issued a paperchase of libel d won the lot hands down.

24

GENIUS,
AND INGREDIENT X

The original concept for the serial which became Coronation Street was, in television terms at least, nothing short of brilliant. But when I inherited the driving seat sixteen years into the series, I began to feel distinctly uncomfortable living with the knowledge that the show's creator had never been properly paid for his work. I took my worries to Granada's top management, and to their credit they instantly agreed the matter had been sadly overlooked. From thereon, the talented writer who invented their money-spinner would share in the rewards.

Tony Warren is a beanpole of a man who cannot talk without flailing his arms like a human windmill. In his company, I would clear a five-square-yard area of drinks, ornaments and any breakables to minimise the damage his animated conversations often caused.

It was Tony, aged twenty-three, and a staff writer in the Granada promotions department, who penned the first twelve episodes of a new drama series he called Florizel Street. He wrote them on an old-fashioned settle in the cosy corner of a pub called the Lantern Pike – the 'local' in his home village of Little Hayfield, in Derbyshire. By strange co-incidence, that same pub, named after a local landmark, is now my own favourite watering hole. I live a stone's throw from the cottage Tony rented at the time of television's most famous creation.

He based Annie Walker on the landlady of the Lantern Pike. She was a formidable, chain-smoking woman called Josephine Paterson, now sadly departed, who was known to friends and foes alike as 'Mrs Pat'. Tony, always a colourful character, must have cut a remarkable figure as he sprawled stomach-down on the settle, scribbling his scripts. Heaven knows what visitors made of it. The regulars were faintly amused by what became a familiar sight. One thing is certain; they could never have guessed they were watching a genius at work and television history in the making.

Before it finally reached the screen, Agnes, the Granada tea lady, was either asked, or freely offered, her opinion on the title. Florizel – the name of a princess Tony recalled from a childhood fairytale – she correctly concluded sounded like a disinfectant; it was removed from the shortlist. But two weeks before the programme was due to make its debut, a name had still not been found. Cecil Bernstein, who had taken the project under his wing, ordered one to be conjured up at the double.

Jubilee Street was considered, and the story is still told of the night the pioneering production team of the three Harrys – Kershaw, Latham and Elton – locked themselves away with two bottles of

Irish whiskey to thrash out the alternatives. Legend has it that Jubilee Street was chosen in drink, and Coronation Street only emerged from the hangover next morning. The rest, as they say, is history. Tony went on to write some two hundred episodes before taking his talents to pastures new. By then he had created a phenomenal success.

As a star staff writer at Granada, earning the princely sum of £30 a week in those early days, Tony was not entitled to any percentages, extras or bonuses even on the strength of the Street's runaway success. Of course, the company's executives were enormously grateful. He was showered with praise for his brainwave; but that didn't exactly pay the rent.

Until Coronation Street appeared, similar programmes had always revolved round middle-class suburbia. Tony based his saga on people who got their hands dirty for a living; a pioneering breakthrough in the world of television. Suddenly millions of working-class British families, many living in mirror-image backstreets, could identify with the Walkers, the Tanners and the Barlows.

Granada's boardroom soon realised they were sitting on a goldmine, and the soaraway success of the show almost guaranteed its sale to nations just starting to experience the television explosion. Sales were not confined to English-speaking countries either. The programme was also exported to an assortment of emergent nations who dubbed or subtitled the Street into a variety of exotic languages. Oddly enough the only people it appeared almost totally lost on were the natives of New York, although one Brooklyn resident wrote to Harry Kershaw saying every single character lived in his apartment block. Perhaps

most New Yorkers just couldn't get to grips with the accent.

Elsewhere, almost without exception, Coronation Street was a hit. It was sold from Bangkok to the plains of Northern Nigeria, providing employment for scores of actors, actresses and technicians. But, after he left the programme in 1964, Coronation Street was not putting a single penny into Tony Warren's bank account.

One of the producer's most important duties is to keep costs down and work within the budget. I had to step slightly out of character, therefore, when I sought permission to pay Tony an unsolicited sum. As I have said, my masters were extremely sympathetic. I truly believe that the non-payment of any reward to Tony was an oversight. For his part, Tony had accepted that as a staff writer he was not legally entitled to anything other than his wages for his ideas and hard work, so he had never bothered to press the point.

He was absolutely thrilled when I told him out of the blue that I had negotiated an annual sum, inflation proofed, to last the life of the serial as a continuing 'thank you' for his original idea. The amount is confidential between Tony and Granada, but it was not calculated to enable Tony to put up his feet and retire to a life of luxury in the south of France. He was too precious a talent for that. Tony is the type who needs to be kept reasonably hungry to sustain his appetite for work, and is well aware of this. Nevertheless, he was delighted that Granada had finally expressed its gratitude in a way which will always help keep the wolf from the door.

Viewers still see his name in the credits after each episode – 'Based on an idea by Tony Warren'. But Tony provided much more than an idea. He created all the original characters, and from the very first moment every single one worked. Jack and Annie Walker, mine hosts at the Rovers; vivacious Elsie Tanner, the outspoken lady with a colourful past, and her wayward son, Dennis; Frank and Ida Barlow, and their sons, David and Ken; the boys' crotchety uncle, old soldier Albert Tatlock and the inimitable Ena Sharples; all conceived with convincing vitality. I know from experience just how difficult it can be to bring one new face into the Street. For Tony to have established an entire neighbourhood from scratch and cemented them all so firmly in the hearts of the nation, was sheer genius.

I like to feel I have played my part in enhancing the group of characters which make up Coronation Street, and in re-introducing the gentle humour which went so strangely missing. I had the final word whenever it came to choosing a new regular. Heaven knows, I didn't always get it right. Whether a new character works is not something which can be calculated, weighed up or written about. It is an intangible, indefinable thing. But when it happens, everyone knows it has happened – writers, producer, director, the whole studio – and, most importantly, the viewer.

It can hinge on a mannerism or a gesture. It can be an inflexion in the voice. It can hang on a simple facial expression or even a posture. Sometimes it can be a combination of any or all of these. I wish I knew the answer. It would be a wonderful resource to bottle and sell to producers the world over. All I could do was hope and pray that I would have my fair share of successes. I believe I did, and there have been some wonderful moments savouring the realisation that 'it' has happened.

Some artists have been touched with

the gift, and thrown it all away. Peter Adamson, Len Fairclough for twenty years, was a classic example. Another was Fred Feast the Rovers' potman, and Peter Armitage, who played Bill Webster all too briefly. Each showed all the signs of having that magical quality which makes a character work.

But for every success there was a failure or two. Some never quite attained that mystical Street credibility. The Clayton family failed to grab the imagination of the viewers, or the scriptwriters, despite my hopes. It wasn't the artists' faults, and neither were the writers to blame. Somehow that indefinable quality never bubbled on to the screen. If they could ever be classed as mistakes, then answers could no doubt be found and lessons learned. But after years of searching for the formula I was still making mistakes. Quite recently I brought in Fanny Carby to play Jack Duckworth's battle-axe of a mother-in-law. Fanny is an accomplished actress, but her character didn't work. We wanted a tough, abrasive performance, but through no fault of Fanny's, it never came together, and what emerged was a grating figure for whom no one had the slightest sympathy. When it doesn't work, it is ultimately the producer's responsibility. But for all the occasions when I have felt like hanging my head in shame, others have given me a tremendous feeling of fulfilment and pride.

Coronation Street currently employs, in almost equal mixture, artists who have come up through provincial theatre and ones who learned their talents on the stages of working-men's clubs. The theatre folk are stage-struck grafters who endured derisory wages, appalling conditions and cheap, cheerless lodgings in search of the public's approval. To them, a well-paid regular job with Coronation Street may well have come as a blessed relief. They often feel a suppressed but understandable resentment towards the cabaret group. After all, what have they suffered for their art?

I occasionally saw it rise to the surface, particularly when non-theatricals found it hard to remember longish tracts of script and resorted to ad-libbing. But the Street really is like a family. They may squabble within, but let the pressure come from outside and ranks will swiftly close. In their heart of hearts, the theatrical brigade would never deny that the likes of Ivy Tilsley, Jack and Vera Duckworth, and Percy Sugden have more than earned their places.

I first spotted the potential of Liz Dawn, who plays loudmouthed Vera to such devastating effect, when she acted as a barmaid in a situation comedy I was producing and directing. Liz only had a smallish part, but she had an unforgettably gushing personality, which again came across in a Formica advert she made shortly afterwards, and made an immediate impact when I introduced her as Vera Duckworth. Liz had done the rounds of the northern cabaret circuit as a singer, only to become an overnight success as an actress.

Jack, played by William Tarmey, had a similar background. Loveable loafer Jack was often referred to by Liz at the Baldwin factory. But he was never seen until the wedding of Brian and Gail Tilsley in 1979. I believe we unearthed a precious jewel when we plucked Bill Tarmey from the obscurity of film extra to create a starring role in the Street.

Fans of gravel-voiced Jack would be surprised at Bill's silver-tongued way with romantic ballads. He had worked as a compère at nightclubs as well as singing on the circuits of British Legion and working-men's clubs. Like many other club artists, as an Equity cardholder Bill could supplement his cabaret earnings working for Granada as an extra. I decided to give him a chance. As Jack Duckworth, hen-pecked hubby, would-be Romeo and loser in life, Bill found fame and fortune. It couldn't have happened to a nicer man. He is now a key figure in the programme. His repartee with Vera, and his losing battle to gain the upper hand with Bet in the Rovers, often provide the comic highlights in the Street.

Unfortunately, Bill fell victim to the pressures of success. In 1987, after he had a complicated heart by-pass operation, I promised to ease him gently back into the show. But the scriptwriters had missed Jack so much, and had so many funny lines stored up for him, they wanted him in every scene. I tried my best to ease his workload, but the guy soldiered on undaunted. Thank goodness he didn't crack up under the strain.

Another comic character I'm delighted to have introduced is Bill Waddington, prickly Percy Sugden. Bill's career goes back to the start of the Second World War. As one of the 'Stars in Battledress' he was billed as 'The army's number one comedian', and he still treasures the memory of his Royal Command Performance in 1955. But when I first saw Bill at Granada he was a warm-up man, entertaining audiences before comedy shows were recorded. Scriptwriter John Stevenson suggested he might be ideal as the new caretaker of the Community Centre. I agreed. Bill grabbed the chance, and revels in his new career.

By making Percy such a colourful character, Bill has helped save the screen life of Emily Bishop. We had been concerned for some time that Emily had

Vera and Jack Duckworth: a perfect match

been heading nowhere and there was every danger she might have disappeared altogether. Actress Eileen Derbyshire has been a valued stalwart since earliest days, but there is no room for sentiment in television drama. Many writers found it hard to invent story-lines for Ernie's widow, and carrying passengers is a luxury a twice-weekly series can ill afford. By moving Percy in as her lodger, the writers found a perfect solution. They make a comic 'odd couple' and I suspect Percy will be the cause of Emily's exasperation for years.

I overruled some scriptwriters when I brought dithering Derek Wilton in on a regular basis. Many thought Derek was acceptable only in small doses, and believed his indecision would be a source of unbearable irritation if it became a permanent feature. I allowed myself to be talked out of a marriage between Derek and the twittering spinster, Mavis Riley, played so beautifully by Thelma Barlow. Viewers may remember the first wedding never took place because both bride and groom got cold feet, and failed to turn up at the church. In fact the cold feet were mine.

I felt almost immediately that I had made a mistake, and vowed to make it second time lucky for actor Peter Bald-

Percy's in trouble, as Emily makes clear

win, who was so keen to join the team. I'm sure the judgement was sound, and I hope Derek's neurotic nature keeps us all entertained in the years ahead.

In my first few months, I concentrated a great deal of attention on the characters and how they slotted into the community's life. It was hard to overlook that one side of the Street was dominated by the burnt-out remains of an old factory. Apart from being an eyesore, it was also an enormous waste of space which hid a golden opportunity to expand the programme.

It was generally agreed that the factory should reopen, which gave me the chance to bring a wideboy Cockney into this northern domain to provide a contrast not only of accent, but of attitude.

The consensus was that we needed a chirpy, streetwise character planning to turn the premises into a base for manufacturing jeans. Denim was all the rage in 1976, and the opening of a little rag-trade factory exactly suited the mood of the show. It also gave us the chance to introduce a whole workforce of new faces.

The casting director suggested Johnny Briggs for the factory boss. I instantly recalled his performances as Inspector Lockhart's sergeant sidekick in No Hiding Place, and thought he was just the job. Johnny accepted the part of Mike Baldwin and within a few weeks we had become firm friends. In real life, Johnny is just as outgoing and full of fun as Mike. He likes a drink, a good laugh and

Derek and Mavis finally tie the knot, with Emily, Rita and Percy

the style of company I like to keep. He also shares Mike's underlying ruthless streak, particularly when it comes to business. It doesn't often bubble to the surface but, like many basically nice people, he thoroughly enjoys himself when he has to pretend to be nasty. After Mike's marriage to the whingeing Sue Barlow broke up, I told him, 'Now we are going to turn you into a thoroughly nasty little piece of work again.' Johnny grinned from ear to ear and said, 'Thank God for that.'

One of the first machinists who came to work for Mike was a plump little lady called Ivy Tilsley. At first, Ivy only appeared from time to time, but Lynne Perrie injected a touch of magic into the role which appealed to me. I decided the

character should be developed. Few people realised that I made her a bigamist when a family was subsequently built around her. Her original husband, Jack, though rarely seen, was played by an actor called Bert Gaunt. There was no death or divorce; he simply faded away. When Ivy, Bert and her son Brian moved into number five, I brought in Peter Dudley to play the dad. Bert Gaunt took a very professional attitude to the breakup of his screen marriage, and simply sent a lighthearted telegram saying that if Ivy didn't mind, he would just call round now and then to claim his conjugal rights.

Poor old Ivy never has much to be lighthearted about. Before joining us, Lynne Perrie appeared in cabaret not only as a singer but also as a very talented comedienne. But, as she has constantly reminded me, Ivy hardly ever utters a comic line. She seems to be constantly caught up in heartbreak and tragedy. Her husband lost his job, was badly injured in a compressor accident, and died some months later. Her son Brian was hardly a source of fun, as his marriage stumbled from one crisis to the next, before his life was finally snuffed out in a backstreet stabbing. Such plots don't lend themselves to the comic repartee Lynne would love to tackle, and I can't imagine that my departure is going to make much difference to the fortunes of the luckless lady she plays. The fans will cry through Ivy's heartbreaks, but I doubt she will ever give them a great deal of laughter.

It takes all sorts to make a rounded drama series, and while I think I've been successful enough in striking a balance between humour and sadness, there was always space between the cobbles and cracked paving slabs for a really poisonous snake to crawl along Coronation Street. In real life, Mark Eden is as nice and gentle a guy as you could wish to meet. But on screen he does make the most wonderful out-and-out baddie.

He first rolled into Coronation Street in 1981 as Wally Randall, the lorry driver who broke Elsie Tanner's heart. Elsie had hoped true love and marriage would blossom, until Wally bluntly gave her the elbow, saying she was too old for romance. It gave Pat Phoenix one of her most memorably poignant scenes, when Elsie, believing she was indeed a wornout old has-been, poured her heart out to Mike Baldwin. It was a magnificent performance, but it was Mark Eden's performance as her hard-hearted seducer which I recalled four years later when I was looking for someone to play

a stone-faced, occasionally tough character called Alan Bradley.

Alan arrived as the estranged father of Jenny Bradley, the newspaper delivery girl Rita Fairclough 'adopted' when her mother died. He made his exit quite recently when Mark made a brilliant job of being charming and loving to Rita while sending out every possible warning signal to viewers about the depth of his sincerity. Scriptwriter Peter Whalley came up with the dramatic scenario which put Bradley behind bars. His suggestion that Alan should use the name of the late-lamented Len Fairclough to obtain a building society loan and set up in the security alarm business was a master-stroke. Coupled with the near-murderous attack on Rita, it meant a jail sentence for the character and, sadly, the disappearance – at least for the time being – of an outstanding actor.

I knew Mark was very happy with the programme, so it was with anything but relish that I broke the news that he would have to go. Mark accepted the decision with complete professionalism, agreeing that the story-line was irresistible. At least it gave him the chance to turn in a series of very meaty performances before he went.

Mark turned Alan Bradley into the most hated man on television, and he thoroughly enjoyed it, although it gave him some uncomfortable moments. He received sackloads of hate mail, and after an incensed lady set about him with an umbrella, Mark thought it prudent to curtail his regular strolls around Manchester. When he did venture out, he had the look of a hunted man, and eyed anyone who recognised him with caution.

Mark was not the first to have played a number of roles in Coronation Street. Roy Barraclough holds the record for the

Rita, Jenny and Alan Bradley; trouble brewing

most speaking parts, and it is a tribute to his splendid acting ability that he can assume the identity of any person he cares to play. I wonder how many viewers spotted him as the underground guide who conducted a Street trip down a network of Derbyshire caves. He then emerged as I-Spy Dwyer, the man who sold Stan Ogden his window-cleaning round. He later became more firmly established as tricky Alec Gilroy, agent to Rita Fairclough in the days of her cabaret singing, and the wheeler-dealer owner of the Graffiti Club. It was never a great problem inducing Roy to make a fleeting visit to Weatherfield. The tough

job was persuading him to stay. While many actors would give their right arm to land a Coronation Street contract, Roy's terrific talent meant he was rarely short of work, either on stage or the more lucrative television, and he was not easily tempted.

Apart from Coronation Street, he will probably he best remembered as the amiable old biddy, Cissy, the other half of Les Dawson's hilarious drag act. Furthermore, as a bachelor, Roy did not have to think about ensuring the security of a family, so that he could more easily resist settling down to a life in the Street. Roy was always reluctant to commit

Alec and Bet enjoy domestic harmony

himself, and had an obsessive fear of becoming typecast as Alec.

After we married him off to Bet Lynch, I still had to muster all my persuasive powers to place Roy's signature on a contract. Even then, I was resigned to losing him when his contract expired in November 1988, just a few weeks before my own retirement. He insisted on leaving before he became better known as Alec Gilroy than Roy Barraclough, and all my efforts to dissuade him failed.

Suddenly, out of the blue, he had a change of heart and the scriptwriters were spared the task of inventing a plausible exit for Bet's tubby hubby. To this day I don't know what brought about the change of mind, but one morning I received a short note from David Liddiment, Granada's commissioning executive for light entertainment: 'Whatever you do, don't proceed with the story-line to write out Roy Barraclough. He is staying.' It was wonderful news. I felt secure in leaving the show at the top of the ratings with the added strength of Alec staying to help take it into a new era. While Alec Gilroy's departure would not have been a fatal blow, both he and Roy Barraclough would have been sadly missed.

Julie Goodyear's natural flair for comedy and Alec's droll, expressive face have produced some memorable moments. Theirs may have seemed an improbable match, but like Emily Bishop and Percy Sugden they make a perfect odd couple, and a fertile area for comedy writing.

Off-screen, Julie and Roy get along famously. Their senses of humour are well-matched, and when they are not affectionately taunting each other they are jointly sending everyone else up. I'm very happy I left the programme with the two still in harness, although I suspect my successor will always have trouble persuading Roy to sign on for another year.

When actress Sue Nicholls made her debut as Audrey Potter in August 1979, I had no idea I was introducing an aristocratic touch to Coronation Street. Audrey appeared just before Gail and Brian's wedding, and was originally envisaged as a minor character, but Sue put a sparkle into the part which made viewers and writers want to see more of her. She was written in and out of the show with regularity, usually arriving during the high and low points of her daughter's marriage, and it was several years before I realised that this bouncy, chummy actress was entitled to be addressed as the Honourable Susan Nicholls. She is, in fact, the daughter of Lord Harmar-Nicholls, the Conservative Peer.

Sue never stands on ceremony. She is a hard-working, fun-loving bachelor girl who made herself extremely popular with all the cast. I particularly liked the vivacity she brought to Audrey, and the idea of allowing her to sink her hooks into Alf Roberts was very attractive. The contrast between the two of them lent all sorts of interesting possibilities to a romantic liaison. Audrey was the flighty spendthrift, a goodtime girl with a colourful past. Alf was penny-conscious, and a cautious stick-in-the-mud.

Once a woman of Audrey's imposing character had decided to get her man she was likely to be more persistent than any Canadian mountie. Staid old grocer Alf was dragged so far out of his shell by Gail's flirtatious mum that he finished up buying a sporty MG roadster simply to impress her. The car was provided by my secretary, then Miss Carole Lancaster, now Mrs Carole Brown, and finally used to drive the love-struck Alf into Audrey's waiting arms. When Audrey borrowed the car and returned with it dented, it led to a moving scene between the irate grocer and his tearful sweetheart. The sight of Alf leading the sobbing Audrey upstairs to his flat to comfort her, and picking up a bottle of brandy on the way, was Coronation Street at its best. No one had to see or hear what happened next.

At the beginning of the next episode their engagement was announced and the couple married in December 1985. Sue Nicholls is now very much at home at the Mini Market with her 'Alfie'. She made a brilliant foil to Ivy Tilsley when their children were going through the trauma of divorce and reconciliation. Now, after Brian's death, I feel there is still plenty of scope for rivalry between the two as they fight for the affections of their grandchildren, Nicky and Sarah Louise. In the background will be the diplomat Alf constantly trying to keep the peace while Don Brennan soothes the ruffled feathers of his wife, Ivy.

I first met Geoff Hinsliffe, who plays Don, when he auditioned for Brass, a comedy series I had the great pleasure of producing for Granada. When Geoff drove into Coronation Street at the wheel of the taxi taking Ivy and Vera to a bingo night celebration of Vera's birthday, no one expected he would appear in more than a couple of episodes. But the idea popped up at a script conference that love could blossom between the widowed Ivy and her cheerful cabby. We tested the romance for three months, and I asked Geoff how he felt about plans for a marriage. He knew that if he was interested I would expect a long-term commitment, and Geoff thought seriously for a long time before agreeing. Lynne Perrie was delighted with our choice of screen husband. I wonder whether she would have been so flattered had she known how long Geoff had taken to say 'yes' to me before 'I do' to her.

To accept a role in Coronation Street is a major decision. The money and security are tempting for most, and the fame is also very pleasant, at least in the early days. It cannot, however, be switched on and off at will. Being recognised can be as tedious as it can be flattering. Star status can sometimes be used to secure the best table in a crowded restaurant, but on the down side is the distinct possibility of stares from every direction. What might have been a whisper from one table rises to a chorus when everyone nudges their partners to ask, 'Isn't that so-and-so from Coronation Street?' Leaving after a lengthy period isn't easy either. Some artists who were written out or killed off more than a decade ago are still asked for autographs under their Coronation Street names. That must be the hardest pill to swallow; all the hassle and none of the cash.

Any actor contemplating a regular role in the Street may also, understandably, fear typecasting. Many former cast members find it difficult to obtain other television work because viewers find it so hard to accept a familiar face in an unfamiliar role. There are, of course, notable exceptions. The late Arthur Lowe, who for so long played that delightful old fusspot Leonard Swindley, had a number of situation-comedy successes, most memorably as Captain Mainwaring in Dad's Army. Kenneth Cope, the Street's wide boy Jed Stone, later surfaced very successfully in Randall and Hopkirk Deceased. Others have found it easier to lose their Coronation Street characters by returning to the theatre while the public's memory fades. A few seem to have disappeared altogether.

One of those was Neville Buswell, who played Deirdre's first husband, Ray Langton. He seemed to vanish off the face of the earth when he quit, and I last heard of him some ten years ago when he was spotted working as a croupier in the casinos of Las Vegas. It seems an odd career-change for a young and talented actor, and certainly proves that Coronation Street is something of a gamble, whether you stay or go.

25

THE NEW GENERATION

When I so reluctantly took over the production chair of Coronation Street I promised David Plowright I would give it my best shot – for one year. When the twelve months were up I went back to his office ostensibly to hand back the reins, secretly hoping he would ask me to stay on. Thankfully he did. The truth was, I was thoroughly enjoying myself and there was never a moment during my thirteen years with the programme when, overall, I didn't derive a tremendous satisfaction and wealth of enjoyment from guiding its future.

I sincerely believe in the theory that everyone should make a career change every five years or so, and I would have stuck to that belief and perhaps bowed out a great deal earlier had Coronation Street not been unique. I would be the first to argue that after five years with one man in control, a programme might well be in need of a fresh injection of talent and ideas. However, there was such an input of creativity from the talented writing team Coronation Street attracted, there was never any danger of it being allowed to grow stale.

Inevitably there comes a time when it seems right to say goodbye. For me, that time came with Granada's offer of early retirement, though I felt many regrets leaving a programme which had dominated so much of my life. When you have worked for so long with the same terrific people, they become a second family; and it was to them I was really saying farewell. But I could walk away with the satisfaction of knowing that the family was in great shape. I felt that we had evolved a near-perfect mixture of characters, a blend of age groups which for years to come would give the writing team immense scope to maintain the Street as television's best-loved product.

Much of the credit for the show's enduring success belongs not only to the stalwarts, household names for years, but also to our 'young ones' – the new generation of Street residents. In almost every case these youngsters were initially given but a fleeting chance to make their mark. They seized the opportunity so effectively they quickly won the loyalty of the fans, giving me the pleasurable task of drawing up permanent contracts.

Norman 'Curly' Watts, for instance, may not be anyone's idea of a heart-throb; he hardly matches up to the handsome hunks of Neighbours or the snappy dressers of Dynasty. Yet Kevin Kennedy has bestowed the character with an affectionate charm which easily holds its own against the obvious sex-appeal of a Jason Donovan or a Michael Nader. We brought him into the show in July 1983, a time of high unemployment and limited job opportunities for school leavers. Norman – soon known to all as

Some of the 'young ones': Shirley, Curly, Martin and Jenny

'Curly' because of Kevin's ramrod-straight hair – was a typical example of that unhappy era.

A bright lad, with an impressive list of GCE passes, Curly had to content himself with the job of dustman, or refuse disposal operative, as he preferred. I was always amused, and quietly flattered, when critics sneered that the Street avoided controversy, or important social issues (surely the fate of school-leavers is one of those). Such charges simply meant that we were achieving our objective with the subtlety intended. I have never believed you can influence people by hitting them over the head, nor that the majority of viewers want to come home from a tough day's work to have politics or heavy social comment rammed down their throats. But it is always possible to pass a worthwhile message across in gentler ways.

We have often been accused of avoiding the question of racial problems. True, we have never moved a coloured family into Coronation Street; I had no intention of introducing a token black just to prove we were not prejudiced. When Lisa Lewis became more prominent as factory machinist Shirley Armitage, it was because of her acting ability, not the colour of her skin. Equally, when we planned her affair with Curly, we deliberately kept the black and white issue well within proportions.

I like to think the most memorable moment of their love affair was its consummation, in the flat above the corner shop. Curly's nervous surrender of his virginity was unforgettable. Insisting it should take place under cover of darkness, and imploring Shirley to switch the light off, he uttered the immortal line: 'It's all right for you. I haven't broken my duck yet.'

I was not prepared for the alarming racial hatred which poured through my letter-box. Several viewers were disgusted that I could have sanctioned such a relationship; none of them had the courage to sign their letters, which speaks volumes. I'm sure the writers of such poisonous words represent a tiny minority of the British people, but even so it is sad and disturbing to realise some people can still cling to such beliefs.

Perhaps I should not have been surprised. In 1979, when Roman Catholic Brian Tilsley married Protestant Gail Potter, I became the focus for a bundle of hate mail from both Eire and Ulster. I was told – again anonymously – that I should never have allowed a mixed marriage to be screened and from the Catholic side came warnings that people were 'out to get' me. I handed the letters over to the police, and nothing came of the threats, but it is amazing to discover first-hand how firmly entrenched some people's prejudices are. No doubt they all regard themselves as good Christians.

As far as it was possible, I ignored these crackpot letters and when Gail and Brian had their problems, and when Shirley and Curly split up, it was for reasons which can afflict any couple rather than those caused by religion or race. I would never have condoned us going too deeply into these areas. There are plenty of documentary programmes dealing with those issues in depth, and little excuse for a twice-weekly drama series to preach to its faithful.

At the time of writing, Lisa has been written out of the show to have a baby. Whether she will return depends on the new producer and his writing team, but I'm confident that Kevin Kennedy will be playing Curly Watts for many years yet. Kevin and his sidekick Kevin Webster, played by Michael le Vell, had a slightly prickly habit of making me feel my age by insisting on calling me 'Boss'. Although I was in overall charge, I hope I never made myself aloof from people, and I was happy for everyone to call me Bill. Whether in deference to my age, or out of old-fashioned respect, Kevin and Michael obviously found it difficult to adopt my Christian name. 'Boss' they chose, and 'Boss' it remained.

They are both extremely nice, well-mannered lads who give every indication of wishing to stay for as long as the programme will have them. Neither of them seems overawed, either by fame or their burgeoning finances. In fact when the Sunday omnibus edition resulted in a hefty pay-rise for the cast, Michael asked how on earth he was going to spend it all. 'Wisely lad,' was the simple answer.

When Kevin's father, played by Peter Armitage, suddenly decided to quit the show, Kevin had already established his own little niche as a spanner-hand in Brian Tilsley's garage, which made it much easier to keep him. I was anxious to do so, because he had brought a special sparkle to the character which had not been lost on our young female fans. In real life he's an 'old' married man now; his wife is actress Janette Bevereley, who became a star herself in the BBC's Sharon and Elsie series.

For some time, Curly and Kevin formed two-thirds of Coronation Street's trio of bachelor boys. The third was Terry Duckworth, tearaway son of Jack and Vera. He arrived in the show in the late summer of 1983, having failed to become an army paratrooper. Terry was always envisaged as a bad lad, and actor Nigel Pivaro was supremely good at capturing the sneering arrogance we were looking for. Terry had a dreadful attitude to women – treat 'em mean, treat 'em tough; love 'em and leave 'em. Neverthe-

less Nigel attracted as fat a sack of fan mail as Michael le Vell, who played the upright young citizen any mother would be pleased to welcome into her daughter's life.

Nigel asked to leave the show after four years to allow him to tour with No Further Cause for Concern, in which he played a convict. I believe he enjoyed the break, although I'm sure it brought home to him just how hard and often financially unrewarding a touring production can be. After a tough year he thoroughly enjoyed playing alongside factory boss Mike Baldwin. Watching wheeler-dealer Mike teaching wide-boy Terry the ropes was like viewing the sorcerer and his apprentice. It was inevitable that when Terry tried to outsmart his tutor, and borrowed his beloved Jag to impress a bird, he would end up with egg on his face. This story-line led to Terry's Street departure for a second time, but he will almost certainly be back.

Terry's second exit coincided with the gradual build-up of the character of Martin Platt, played by Sean Wilson. Martin's role as one of life's young drifters is easily recognisable. He seems destined to spend his youth between the dole queue and casual work, feeling slightly hard done by, and waiting for a fairy Godmother to change his luck. There's plenty of time for Martin to grow up and settle down. Perhaps the script-writers will eventually pair him off with Jenny Bradley, although I can't help feeling she is destined for someone with a little more substance than her friend Martin.

Sally Ann Matthews arrived as fourteen-year-old paper girl Jenny in 1984, and her character has grown immensely. What amazes me about Sally, together with all the other Coronation Street youngsters who have found fame so early in their lives, is the way she handles it. None of them have allowed it to go to their heads. Sally Ann is a charming, lovely girl who enjoys horse-riding in the hills around her native Oldham and her behaviour is a sharp contrast to another young actress who many years ago allowed her success in the Street to wreck her life.

I refer to poor Jenny Moss, who played Lucille Hewitt in the late sixties and was long gone before I took over as producer. Jenny simply couldn't handle the life of a celebrity and her world took a fast downhill spiral through heavy drinking and five marriages. Thankfully it appears that Jenny, now a grandmother, is back on her feet after all those wasted years. I'm just grateful that none of the Street's younger generation who came under my wing have ever given me cause for great anxiety.

I did, however, get concerned about our tiniest stars. In its twenty-ninth year, and as popular as ever, who would lay bets that Coronation Street will not survive the century? It is not beyond the realms of possibility for a baby to join the Street and play a character from cradle to the grave. This possibility raises all sorts of moral issues, and I for one do not know the answers. As it is without precedent, there is no way to form a considered judgement on the likely consequences of a child growing up with two separate or, viewed differently, totally intertwined, identities. If this is going to happen to anyone, I would guess young Warren Jackson is likely to be the first.

I first set eyes on Warren in a carrycot on my desk. Chris Quinten had carried him in to show me the little chap he wanted to play his son. In the script Gail was expecting a baby and Chris knew I was on the lookout for a newborn child.

Warren Jackson early in his career

Chris was friendly with a couple who had just been blessed with a blonde-haired baby boy and asked them if they would allow him to make a television debut as Nicky Tilsley. The couple were delighted with the idea, and Chris brought the would-be star into my office for an audition. He was a lovely little fellow and after I chatted to his parents I was more than happy to award the infant a contract.

Warren Jackson has since won the hearts of the entire cast and grown up with the set as his playground. He's a natural performer who, on the basis of his present performance, as an actor and a child growing up, could well be allowed to go on playing the part into adulthood. But I can't help asking myself whether he might one day start wondering if he is really living the life of Warren

The christening of Tracy Langton

Jackson, or of his character Nicky.

Perhaps it is a little soon to start worrying about Warren, but I did have cause to express deep concern about the future of another youngster who was heading for a lifetime career in the Street. Christobel Finch played Tracy Langton, later adopted as Tracy Barlow, for the first six-and-a-half years of her life. I had several talks with Christobel's father, Ken Finch, about the dangers I foresaw in his daughter continuing to live with the character. I warned him that it could, for all I knew, have a detrimental effect on her psychologically. Ken Finch thanked me for my concern, but felt sure his daughter was thoroughly enjoying her role and having no problems in any other direction.

The situation resolved itself in a totally unexpected fashion. Mr Finch had business problems and came under a lot of pressure. Without a word to me, he moved his family to Guernsey, and Christobel never appeared as Tracy Barlow again. One problem was solved, but I was now faced with another. If I went in immediate search of a replacement, the youngster would have to look very like Christobel. I felt we could risk another tack. At that age, children's appearances often change significantly, and we decided it would be some months before Tracy was seen again. In the script she would either be out playing, upstairs in bed or staying with relatives. The plot worked remarkably well. Tracy turned into something of a little phantom, but when she finally re-emerged on screen no one was surprised by the appearance of schoolgirl actress Holly Chamarette.

Only the press gave us any problem. Tracy, in the form of Christobel, had last been seen in September 1983, and was reincarnated as Holly almost two years later in July 1985. In the meantime, some TV critics asked tongue-in-cheek whether Tracy had been kidnapped. As far as the programme was concerned, their questions were largely ignored. Coronation Street has always kept the roles of its child actors low-key, and prolonged absences are not often remarked on by viewers. I'm convinced that the missing Tracy only drew mischievous comments from the press because they felt Christobel's sudden emigration had caught us unprepared.

Her record as the longest appearance from infant to child has been overtaken by Warren, who, at the time of writing, has been nine years with the show. Though he has grown with the part, I had decided that it wouldn't be wise to allow Holly to play Tracy for too long. She might have a brilliant career ahead as a doctor or a lawyer. It seemed wrong that she might consider her career mapped out, from such an early age, as Tracy Barlow. So Holly made her final appearance in March 1988, and Dawn Acton took over the following December. She was to be the last Street debutante of my era.

There was one other Street baby whose short life reduced us all to tears. Little Leah King was chosen for the role of Sarah Louise Tilsley, simply because she was born in the right place at the right time. Gail was filming her make-believe birth three weeks after Leah and her twin sister Linsay had been safely delivered in the same Manchester hospi-tal. Their parents, devoted Street fans, happily agreed that Leah should start her life as an infant actress, and she was the lustily healthy baby gently placed in Gail's arms. Helen Worth thought the world of her 'adopted' child, and was heartbroken when Leah died tragically four months later from cot death syndrome.

There was never any suggestion that Leah's appearances in the programme contributed to her death, but we were all very unsure of what to say to her parents other than to express our deepest sorrow. We all knew that sooner or later a second Sarah Louise would have to be found, and eventually it was decided to ask the Kings how they felt about Linsay taking over. To our great relief the family were in no way offended. On the contrary, they were pleased to have been asked because they had already discussed the possibility, and felt that for the sake of Leah's memory the decision was right.

Linsay has now grown beyond the age considered dangerous for cot deaths, but for months her cradle was wired with sophisticated electronic alarms which monitored her heartbeat and breathing. One of the most touching things was that for some weeks after her twin's death, Linsay would only settle to sleep with a baby-sized doll in the cot next to her. The sight and feel of the substitute was a comfort for Linsay, although for everyone else it was a painful reminder of the tragedy which engulfed the programme. I think Leah's parents made an immensely brave decision. The programme will no doubt always remind them of their great loss, but somehow they have managed to balance this out by remaining very much involved in its production.

Peeping into Coronation Street – fans queue to look through a specially cut window in the outdoor set

26

THE CREATIVE PROCESS,
AND A MOLE UNEARTHED

The making of Coronation Street revolves around a precise twenty-one-day cycle, sparked by a new beginning every third Monday. This is the day the producer meets with the team of ten regular writers, two story associates and secretary, to dream up and write down enough story ideas to fill the next six episodes. It was also the day I feared most. Invariably, Monday morning's approach swamped the preceding weekend in a sea of nervous tension, and I rarely opened the meeting without a racing pulse and a churning stomach. I always went armed with a good joke to break the tension, and a pack of antacid tablets to survive the day.

Originally the story conference was held in Room 600, Granada's boardroom, but later we moved to the less imposing atmosphere of a studio committee room or, when that wasn't available, a conference suite at a city hotel. But whatever the venue, the problem stubbornly remained the same.

We went in at ten-thirty, knowing we must emerge in the late afternoon with enough ideas and information to fill three hours of television. The prospect was daunting. No matter how well the ideas appeared to be flowing, there was always the nagging fear that one day we wouldn't manage to prepare enough information for the story associates to turn their notes into a working synopsis

for the next three weeks. The writers shared this responsibility. Without a synopsis of each episode they could not turn their ideas into a working script. These meetings were rarely gentlemanly affairs; but if they had ever grown into a cosy little club which reached instant agreement on a polite show of hands, I suspect Coronation Street would soon have died.

We normally kicked off pleasantly enough with coffee and a wide-ranging debate, covering anything from what the papers had been saying recently about the programme, to where each of the six previous episodes had stood in the ratings. But after fifteen minutes of chat it was time to get down to serious business.

Usually there are two main story-lines running through any one episode, with the thread of a third gradually developing. There were always a few stories inherited from the previous meeting which, according to their level of importance, would continue running through the next three weeks. The first job was always to pick up these stories and either discuss their progress during the current episodes, or decide when they would reach a conclusion. Once this was completed, we could turn our attention to something new.

This was usually where the fireworks started. Writers are naturally creative people, and when ten are put under pressure around a table there is bound to be some form of explosion. I never presided over a story conference where there wasn't some degree of hair-tearing and shouting. Our team were a generous mix of individuals who, in their moments of frustration, would all react in different ways. As the arguments swayed the mood one way, then the other, some would go into a silent sulk; others would leap out of their chairs, beating the tables with their fists. I was referee, judging the right moment to blow the whistle.

Eventually the outburst would subside, but of course at that precise moment someone in the wings would choose to make some flippant remark and fuel an even greater row. They never quite came to blows, although there were some moments during screaming matches when everyone held their breath. Walkouts were not uncommon. Sometimes they lasted only minutes while someone took a grip on their frustrations by walking the corridors. Just occasionally they could last until lunchtime, when a few beers would quench the fires.

After a major walkout, it was always entertaining to guess how long the protest would last. Some purposely set out to needle each other. You could often see it coming and pray they would keep their mouths shut. They rarely did. Little rows blazed merrily across various points of the table. For the most part I let them get on with it. As long as the stories were coming, there were always entertaining moments to lighten the fiercest bust up.

Although I ran a fairly democratic organisation the final word would rest with me. Having listened to all the arguments and often a fair degree of histrionics, there would come a time when I had to put my foot down and dictate which way a story would go, knowing full well this was bound to upset some people on the right of the table and delight others on the left.

I tried experiments to ease the pressure. I paired off writers, asking them to spend the occasional day together in an effort to generate story ideas. I don't know why the experiment never quite worked, except that, with a few exceptions, writers prefer to operate alone.

Probably the best safety valve we created was the long-term planning conference. We would book a hotel room every three or four months and, with the reward of a good lunch and fine wine in view, sit down to our long-term story planning relaxed in the knowledge that there was no pressure to produce the outlines of six scripts by the evening. We refined this idea to a point where we held them every couple of months, and towards the end of my term the actual story conference had become a much more relaxed forum where the only real job was to put flesh on the bones of plots which had already been outlined. It didn't stop blood pressures getting a little high at times, but at least the meetings seemed better-natured, and I could sit back and enjoy them.

The tears and tempers were balanced by tremendous humour and fun. Years of experience had taught our band of writers that there were more ways than one to skin a cat. Often, after an idea had been thrown out, they would plot to craftily resurrect it under a different guise. I had to be very alert to spot the camouflage, and blue-pencil any attempt at a sneaky re-entry by the back door.

Coronation Street has an enormous appetite for stories and as the long day wore on, an idea had to be pretty outrageous not to be given a thorough hearing. Some brainwaves had all the hallmarks of late-afternoon specials. These were the story-lines swiftly awarded a rejection slip in the morning, but which suddenly acquired more appeal as four-o'clock passed and we were nowhere near filling our assignment of six scripts. The idea would be back on the table, perhaps with an extra ingredient, or a new angle, which made the story acceptable, if only just. The passage of time never redeemed these decisions. Three months later, after their transmission, we would look at each other and say, 'That must have been a four-thirty job.'

Some were consigned to the repertoire of four-thirty jokes. John Stevenson once dreamed up the highly unlikely story of Emily Bishop having a secret drink problem. It was so outrageous and caused such a laugh that he trotted it out regularly to revive flagging spirits. But then, the suggestion was made long before Percy Sugden became Emily's lodger. The longer he stays the more realistic the idea becomes. If viewers ever see Percy puzzling over empty sherry bottles in the dustbin they will know John's idea has finally taken wing.

Very often the little ideas made the best television. As I have said, one of my first tasks was to rediscover the Street's humour, and Peter Tonkinson, then a full-time story associate, presented me with a little gem. He suggested Albert Tatlock and Stan Ogden should be accidentally locked overnight in the cellar of the Rovers. It was simple, neat and plausible. But most important, when the drunken pair were discovered the next morning, it was extremely funny.

Another classic little story in the same mould actually came from a viewer, who suggested Eddie Yeats should keep chickens in the Ogdens' back yard. The story-line as originally suggested was not acceptable, but with a little thought we turned the idea into a lot of fun. Stan and Eddie were constantly on the look-out for any scheme involving maximum profit from the minimum of work, and the thought of eggs by the dozen would surely appeal to their entrepreneurial spirit. To give the story extra spice the hens were installed while the long-suffering Hilda was away. The punch-line came on her return. Her face was a picture when she discovered her home was a shambles, topped off by a broody hen sitting as the centre-piece to her kitchen table.

It is relatively easy to arrange a series of disasters, deaths and dramas, but a constant diet of these would never work. They have their place, but Coronation Street is really a carefully woven quilt of little human stories full of humour and sometimes pathos. The ideas for these are always more difficult to find.

Just occasionally I accepted an idea then wished I hadn't. One such regret was making Deirdre Barlow a councillor. I was never happy about it, although I allowed myself to be persuaded. Certainly it provided a fertile patch for the writers to dig into, but I still find it slightly incredible that someone of Deirdre's character would want to represent her community on the local council.

For the most part politics and religion were taboo, and we had to keep an eye open to avoid being drawn into a major controversy. With upwards of twenty-five million viewers I imagine we could even have influenced the outcome of a general election. If one of the more serious-minded characters like Ken Barlow had strategically voiced his support for one or other party, we might easily have thrown the poll predictions into chaos.

A little surprise for Hilda

As a rule, our soapbox stands were kept at a more parochial level. Harry Kershaw made entertaining attempts to kick over the traces. If he ever came across a barrier of red tape, whether from the inland revenue, council planners or the mandarins of Whitehall, Harry would craftily try to work his beef into the script. The Post Office lived in terror of Harry's pen. He was always gleefully ready to charge out righting whatever wrongs crossed his path, and parts of his scripts often had to be returned to him, heavily blue-pencilled.

When the Roman Catholic Tilsley family moved in, it sparked some strong reactions, especially from Northern Ireland. Some viewers objected to the crucifix displayed on their wall. There was even greater outrage from the Province when we gave our blessing to the mixed marriage between Gail and Brian.

It was a constant battle to keep a contrasting balance of stories running through each episode. Ideally, we wanted a degree of romance, drama and comedy in each one, but that was not always possible. Sometimes one of the three had to take precedence. The episodes which dealt with the shooting of Ernie Bishop, and more lately the stabbing of Chris Quinten, were classic examples; pure drama drove everything else into the background. The slightest thread of comedy would have been totally insensitive.

Although Coronation Street has touched on social comment, I never allowed the programme to become a platform for debate, moral or otherwise. I regard that as the province of documentary, not light entertainment. East Enders took up the cudgels for just about every controversial issue, from homosexuality and AIDS to drug addiction. The serial seems to plunge from one depress-ion to the next. When I first heard of the BBC's plans to launch a rival I thought it had hit on a good idea. Cockney wit and humour are powerful indeed. I find it staggering that the programme never attempted to reflect it; comedy and general humour are such essential ingredients to the long-running success of Coronation Street. If the BBC asked me to take over EastEnders, humour would be the first thing I would inject. However, it will be interesting to see how long the programme survives.

As a direct competitor, EastEnders never held any great fears, but we felt deeply frustrated when it was wrongly shown to have overtaken us as Britain's most popular programme. The viewing figures were always misleading. We knew our individual figures for Monday and Wednesday were much higher than theirs for Tuesday and Thursday, but when EastEnders added the viewers they captured for their Sunday omnibus it gave them a substantial lead. It was only after Coronation Street launched its own weekend omnibus that we began batting on the same wicket and the true picture emerged.

The one thing the two programmes have in common is the unrelenting scrutiny of the popular press and a constant leak of the best story-lines. Security was a major headache for Coronation Street. No matter how hard we tried to keep our story ideas under wraps, the press always seemed to discover our plans. There is a great debate whether advance publicity generates more interest in the programme, or simply spoils the entertainment value. There are arguments for both, but I can think of a number of story leaks which made me very angry. One which particularly springs to mind involved Len and Rita before they married. Rita had decided there would be no wedding and was heading off for Tenerife to resume her cabaret-singing career. The scene was set at Manchester airport where a woeful Len was seeing her off for the whole summer. Rita's flight was called and she disappeared to the appropriate gate. The punchline came when viewers discovered that in a sudden and romantic change of heart, Rita had purposely missed the flight and set her wedding bells ringing. It would have been a wonderful surprise for millions if someone hadn't leaked the story to the national press. The plot was ruined and lost every ounce of impact.

We long suspected we had at least one major mole within the Granada organisation and possibly a few minor ones too. But when our most diligent betrayer was finally unmasked, it was a bitter blow. She was discovered at the heart of the production team, and it is hard to calculate how much grief and damage she caused over the years. For a long time the finger of suspicion had pointed very near the centre of our organisation. The suggestion seemed unthinkable, but as more and more stories were leaked, the trail appeared to lead to Esther Rose, one of the two story associates who knew every detail of our forward planning. I imagine that trapping a clever spy is an immensely difficult and painstaking task, although Esther might have been unmasked much earlier if there had been a greater will on my part. I had thought of planting false information which only the two of us would share, but I could never come up with a foolproof scheme. All ideas were formulated at the story-planning conferences, which always involved at least fifteen people. It was a heavy cloak to hide behind, and Esther had for years concealed her betrayal in its folds.

Finally she made a fatal mistake. The great disappointment for us was that she let her guard slip only two days before she retired. Had we caught her earlier it would have given me great satisfaction to give her the boot. Mervyn Watson, who took over from me, overheard Esther making a telephone call. Through an office door she had carelessly left open, he heard her speaking at dictation speed to some newspaper contact giving personal information and the home address of Liz Dawn and her husband. At the time, the actress who plays Vera Duckworth was going through a domestic crisis and the detail Esther was relaying was hot news.

I called her into Mervyn's office the following morning and laid the charge before her. She denied any knowledge, but I had all the proof I needed. I told her, 'It's just a pity your retirement is so near. If you weren't going tomorrow you would certainly be fired.'

Everyone within Coronation Street knew I wouldn't tolerate the leaking of advance story-lines. If some member of the cast or production team let something slip in an unguarded moment, or at a party where a little too much drink had been taken, then at least it was understandable. For a trusted, well-paid colleague to sell the information in cold blood was unforgiveable.

Esther heaped trouble on the programme long after she had left. She gave the press a story which supposedly involved the calling of a top-secret meeting to devise a suitable way to kill off the whole programme. According to her, the production team and writers had secretly hired a room at the Midland to discuss the final details, while along the road Granada's board of directors had gathered to ratify the decision. It was pure fiction. We had indeed hired a room at the Midland – for one of our regular forward-planning conferences. It was merely coincidence that the board were meeting at the same time.

There has never been as much as a suggestion to kill off the programme. It was a ludicrous story. Coronation Street's place at the top of the ratings spells out the programme's continuing popularity, and no one would think of killing the goose which lays the golden eggs. Every television organisation in the country would love to have the programme on its billings; even Southern companies freely admit that, despite its distinct Northern flavour, the serial is immensely popular in their regions. Should the programme ever go into serious decline and slip disastrously down the ratings, then I think it should be taken off the air, out of respect. Coronation Street has meant so much to so many for so long that I don't think anyone would want to watch it die slowly. That, however, is not happening; quite frankly I don't think it will in the foreseeable future.

Hard work and dedication to the series has meant that Coronation Street has won award after award over the years

27

BEHIND THE SCENES

The first rehearsals for Coronation Street generally begin just after lunch on Monday in an atmosphere even more make-believe than the actual programme. Technicians armed with different-coloured sticky tape mark out the walls of a make-believe pub on the rehearsal room floor and everyone pretends it's the Rovers. Jack Duckworth humps crates, heavy only in his imagination. Around the corner, Rita Fairclough tidies imaginary magazines on a rack which isn't there, while down the road at number 5, Ivy Tilsley pours Vera a brew from a non-existent tea-pot. There may be the odd chair, and sometimes a table is hauled in as a reference point in the stark and otherwise featureless rehearsal area. But for the most part, the landmarks and living-rooms of Coronation Street are all in the mind. Blocking has begun. This is the technical tag given to the first rehearsal for the two episodes which will be filmed, or more accurately recorded on video tape, at the end of the week.

There is a popular belief that the cast turns up on set for half-an-hour's work on Monday and Wednesday evenings, then melts away again into the glamorous world of show business. The truth is less romantic. Coronation Street is planned down to the last second of the twenty-four-and-a-half minutes which each episode lasts, and every detail of the script and camera work is checked minutely to make sure it all fits in.

If there is outside filming to be done, either on the Street's outside set or some other location in Weatherfield, the cast are up with the sparrows on Monday morning. But at two-thirty prompt that afternoon, the director will expect them to be assembled for his first rehearsal of the week.

The programme has three directors, and each will be at different stages of preparing the two episodes assigned to them during any given three-week period. Each director has had a copy of the script for at least two weeks when he calls the cast to rehearsal, and on the Monday afternoon will mark out the movements and positions the artists are to take in their respective sets.

The cast will have been given copies of the week's two scripts on the previous Wednesday. They will have glanced through them, if only to assess their own involvement, but on Monday they are not expected to have learned their lines. Monday's blocking is primarily to allow the director to work his way through the episodes scene by scene and, as the cast read from scripts, he will direct the movements they are expected to be making. It's hard work; sheer graft in fact.

Emily might be ironing, or Mavis standing, hands clasped, gazing with awe into the eyes of her beloved Derek.

Bill Podmore takes Julie Goodyear, Betty Driver and Doris Speed through an early rehearsal (Photo: News of the World)

Whatever their movements, the director has them written down on the script, along with the camera angles planned for the final filming.

There is little room for mistakes. Later in the week a whole team of cameramen and technicians, fighting against the clock, will be relying on its accuracy. At every stage of the filming the cameraman, in particular, will want to know whether he is shooting in close-up, lining up his camera over some other artist's shoulder, or taking a wide-angled shot of the scene. It isn't left to chance whether he chooses to capture the doting sparkle in Mavis's eyes or the smug self-satisfaction creeping over Derek's face.

Some of the cast, and the old hands in particular, have an uncanny knack of knowing just where and when the director wants them to move. I suppose they have done it so often they learn all the permutations. When I was first asked to direct a couple of episodes, there was a scene in the Tanner household where I could have sworn Pat Phoenix was reading my mind. As a newcomer, I was completely amazed, but Pat explained that now and again she knew instinctively what to do.

By Monday night the blocking will be complete, and on Tuesday morning the cast will assemble for rehearsals which concentrate more on their performances rather than technical events. In the green room there is an atmosphere of hushed concentration. Some artists are huddled in their cubicles committing their lines to memory, others pair off to work together and it's not unusual to find one or more pacing the corridor mumbling away to themselves. The only interruptions tolerated are when the assistant stage manager calls them into the rehearsal room to go through their scenes. As often as not, the majority will still be reading from scripts, but by the afternoon the paperwork is beginning to be discarded, and Monday's basic rehearsal starts to be polished from memory.

Some learn lines much quicker than others. A lot are exceptionally good, but Anne Kirkbride appears to have the wonderful gift of an almost photographic memory. She can read through a page of dialogue and almost instantly know it by heart. Some, however, really struggle. Bill Waddington, who plays Percy Sugden, would be the first to admit he has to work very hard to memorise his script. Then the job becomes nerve-racking and difficult, and the worry sometimes creeps through into the programme. Percy's words sometimes get slightly mixed up. On occasions the mistake is allowed to pass; sometimes the scene must be shot again. That is the moment everyone dreads. They are always sensitive to the fact that their mistake has involved a retake, not only for them, but for everyone else.

In its earliest days, the programme went out live on a Friday night, and the cast went on immediately to tele-record the episode for transmission the following Monday. If mistakes were made, there was little hope of patching anything up. Video recording ended the nightmare of putting out a live drama show, but in the early days there were no tape-editing facilities. Once the recording had started, half the episode had to be completed before they were stopped for the welcome interruption of a commercial break.

Everyone hated to be in the last scene of either half because if anyone made a mistake the entire half-programme had to be recorded over again. Some of the cast inevitably wound themselves up into a near panic worrying about letting everyone down. If someone like dear old

Margot Bryant was in the final scene, the whole cast would almost go down on their knees praying she would make it to the end without fluffing. Despite everyone's care and concern, we often had to film the whole programme twice, and on very black days maybe three times.

When the show was live, the only slight safety net was a dead button held by the assistant stage manager. If someone dried and couldn't deliver a line the sound could be instantly cut off the air, and a prompt would be shouted before the button was released. It was an art in itself to recover the timing, and if things went hopelessly wrong, a tongue-tied actor had no alternative but to ad lib his way out of trouble and hope no one noticed. That is not quite as frightening as it sounds. Very often the actor would know what he was expected to say, but just couldn't remember the words as written.

By a mixture of precise timing, breathtaking courage and a lot of skill, location film had sometimes to be slotted into the live performance being transmitted from the studio. The film would be stationary and ready to roll on a tele-cine machine, but its one great drawback was the six seconds it took from the moment of switch-on, to the point where it reached its operating speed. The production assistant would roll the film for its six-second warm-up, and at the precise moment the programme would cut from studio. To film was hair-raising stuff, and quite often you would signal to an actor to speed up or slow down the delivery of their lines to coincide with the moment when the camera switched. At the end of the pre-recorded film, there would be another countdown of 'ten, nine, eight, seven, six,' and so on, until the cry came 'cue studio' and the action was back live once more.

Once, when I was hauled in at very short notice to direct a couple of episodes when the director assigned had fallen ill, the technical supervisor suggested I might like to take some strain out of the operation by rehearse-recording the scenes. This technique was quite new to Coronation Street. It meant that each scene was rehearsed two or three times to make sure everyone, including the sound engineers and cameramen, had it right, then we instantly went on to record it. For the first time, the whole two episodes were put together in a series of little takes.

The cast loved it, and not long afterwards it was adopted as standard practice. It made such a difference, particularly for more senior members of cast like Violet Carson and Jack Howarth. At last they didn't have to run from scene to scene, recalling their lines on the way.

Later, when I was producer, a director came to me and said, 'I would like to go back to doing it as we did in the old days.'

I looked at him perplexed, wondering whether he was the full shilling. To have returned to the continuous recording technique, as he was suggesting, would have caused a riot.

Recordings begin on Thursday afternoon and continue right through Friday, but before that can happen there is a great deal more work to be done.

By the time Tuesday afternoon's rehearsals have come to a close around five-thirty, the production team has a reasonable idea of how long each episode is running. The networks allow a little flexibility to the twenty-four-and-a-half minutes allotted, but it is only a matter of a few seconds. Even at this relatively early stage, if an episode is running as much as two or three minutes over, or, even worse, under, it would be seen as a serious problem. The writer of the episode would be called in first, to make cuts or write another scene to fill in the gap. If he cannot be reached quickly, the job falls to the producer.

Rehearsals continue on Wednesday morning, but just after lunch Coronation Street begins what is known as the technical run. All artists are called to the rehearsal room, and for many of them it will be the first time they have watched scenes which run alongside their own. Assembled with them are the technical supervisor, the senior cameraman, the sound man, production assistants, ASMs, wardrobe staff, make-up people, props men and stage hands, all observing, and gathering information relevant to their particular jobs. As the week goes on Coronation Street gathers pace, and gathers more and more people to help with its making. By Friday evening the programme will have touched the working lives of hundreds and involved scores in its actual production.

The technical run also gives the artists their first audience of the week. It may be a small one, but there will always be a reaction to something funny, and laughter helps generate confidence. On the other hand, when a scene is particularly charged with emotion it leaves everyone with the creepy feeling they have been caught eavesdropping on private grief. There is always a slight atmosphere of embarrassment until the actors defuse it by shouting something outrageous like, 'He had it coming, anyway.'

By the end of the afternoon, the timing of each scene will have been checked and double-checked. The cast then retreat to the green room for coffee and sandwiches while they wait to hear the good news or the bad. If the timings are still over, some unlucky souls, perhaps

with only a couple of lines in one small scene, can find themselves cut from the episode altogether. If it's still running under, a new scene is quickly rehearsed and patched in.

During the week the required interiors of Coronation Street will be built as they have been week after week, month after month, for almost thirty years. The Rovers dominates the top left-hand corner of the studio as the only part of the set which isn't demolished at the end of each week to make room for other shows. But from there on, few things are geographically correct. One week Alf's shop might, for convenience sake, be constructed right next door to the Kabin. Deirdre's living-room might have moved two doors and end up adjoining Rita's kitchen. If Rita's home is not needed one week, it will not be built at all. It doesn't matter in what order they are constructed. All exterior shots are filmed on the permanent outdoor lot. But once inside those cosy little homes it is of no consequence if number 13 isn't next to number 11, and clever camera angles hide the fact there is only a flimsy plywood wall where Hilda's famous flight of ducks once took wing across her 'muriel'.

But what is vital is the placing of props. Paintings and vases all have their precise position in certain homes, and it would never do for the Websters' dining table to make a quick flit to someone else's house.

The men who dress the set rely to a great extent on memory to get everything right. But for a set which might not have been used for some weeks, there are folios of 10 x 8 photographs to help make sure the continuity is correct.

First thing on Thursday afternoon, every item, from Ken Barlow's briefcase, to the change in Mike Baldwin's pocket,

The original studio set – pavement and cobbles painted on the floor. There was only room to build half the Street for each episode

is checked by the props man before recording can begin. But one day, when Harry Cavanagh was in charge, his sheaf of notes went missing. At first he suspected they had simply been misplaced. But when after a quick glance around the studio they were not to be found, he asked for help in the search. The mystery of the missing papers deepened as the minutes ticked by. Without them, recording simply could not start. To halt a studio is a serious matter; far too many people are involved, and far too much money is at stake. After half an hour the hunt was becoming frantic.

Suddenly Pat Phoenix burst in and threw herself at Harry's feet pleading forgiveness. She had dropped her script on top of the notes, and innocently waltzed off with the lot.

Thursday morning is often set aside for any outdoor filming which couldn't be completed on Monday, but if none is taking place the artists are called at various times to take their place in make-up. Some need more attention than others. Only Jean Alexander needed none at all.

Recording begins at 2.30 p.m., when the studio is manned and the director checks with the floor manager that everything is OK to start rehearsal of the first scene. If extras are required, perhaps for a scene in the Rovers' bar, they will have been placed in position, maybe playing darts, having a drink or a chat, and told their cues to leave or enter the pub. After a couple of rehearsals, the engineer in the main video-tape recording area, far removed from the studio, will be put on standby. The production assistant will check that the director is ready and then cue tape and alert the studio there are ten seconds to the moment recording starts. If all goes well, it's on to the next scene. If not, all or part of the scene will be shot again.

By the end of Thursday afternoon, the director will have calculated how much should have been recorded, always hoping to be ahead of schedule. The whole merry-go-round starts again on Friday morning and if it's a heavy week in studio, both the director and producer will be keeping a nervous eye on the clock. It all has to be in the can by 6.30 that evening. After the weekend, the director and his production assistant shut themselves away in the editing suite to piece together the two episodes. Studio and location video are linked and this is followed by a sound dubbing session where the sound effects are superimposed on the main sound track. From all this hectic precision, Coronation Street emerges – some weeks, I suspect, only by a miracle.

Of course, now that the programme is transmitted three times a week, the work schedule has become even more hectic to accommodate the extra work load, and its not unusual for the Coronation Street team – actors and camera-crew – to work seven days a week.

A multitude of problems present themselves to the producer. Apart from adopting the whole family of Coronation Street and caring for their individual problems, the producer has a responsibility to the millions of viewers who are constantly telephoning and writing.

'Is Brian Tilsley's garage still for sale, as I am very interested?' 'Are there any jobs going in Mike Baldwin's factory? We are good workers and won't let him down.' 'Can I be this, that or the other in Coronation Street?' 'What you need in the Rovers . . .' 'Wouldn't it be a good idea if . . .'

When the postman walks down Coronation Street, he brings a mixed bag.

Letters from fans ask for autographs, for details of clothes worn in the show, even for advice on personal problems. Where possible, they are all answered. Letters from Members of Parliament, teachers, clergymen and organisations ask for support in their current campaigns, or occasionally accuse the programme of setting a bad example. When decimal currency was introduced, the Treasury asked for our support and the then rather peculiar-looking fifty-pence piece was handed over the bar of the Rovers by a bemused Len Fairclough. In the wings was the man from Whitehall waiting to whisk the treasured coin back to London. Considering the Street had given the government a free advertising plug which might otherwise have cost a fortune, they might well have been expected to make us a present of the money. Their courier was accused of downright meanness until it was discovered that, by law, the Treasury is not allowed to give away money in any circumstances.

The actors, too, have a pretty constant flow of mail, but when their characters are involved in controversial story-lines, that steady stream can turn into a torrent.

When Susan Barlow first fell in love with Mike Baldwin, actress Wendy Jane Walker received much unsolicited advice. At the start of the romance, about 25% of the letters said Susan should follow her heart, while 75% forcefully cautioned, 'Beware, he's too old for you, he's got a past, and it will all end in tears.' But as viewers realised that Mike was genuinely in love with Susan and really wanted to make her happy, the pendulum swung in the other direction until, just before the wedding, only a handful were against the marriage, and the vast majority wished the couple lots

of happiness.

Weddings always trigger off a bulging postbag. Viewers write for invitations, slices of wedding cake, or decorations from the top of it. Parents offer their little daughters as bridesmaids and girls planning their own weddings want to know where the Coronation Street bride bought her dress. 'It's exactly the sort of style and colour I've been looking for.'

When Sally Seddon married Kevin Webster, her peach satin dress and jacket brought in dozens of enquiries. A host of disappointed brides had to be told the outfit wasn't available in the shops. It had been made in Granada's costume department. Others, like the one Marion wore when she married Eddie Yeats, were bought off the peg in Manchester and led to a great many copies going proudly down the aisles of churches all over Britain.

Letters come from all corners of the country. A request arrived from Dorset for election posters of Alf Roberts and Deirdre Barlow. The viewer promised equal space for each in the windows of her home. From Blackpool came the information, 'My Afghan hound, Claude, has always, since he was born, sung the theme tune of Coronation Street.' From the Midlands the staff of a marriage bureau wrote offering to find a husband for Bet Lynch.

The Street gets international mail, too. A Dutch couple living on New Zealand's Great Barrier Island wrote to say they had managed to keep up with life in the Street by running their television off a twelve-volt car battery.

When barmaid Gloria Todd was confronted by her Canadian half-brother, who wanted to reconcile her with her mother, a viewer called Gloria wrote to confide, 'That episode knocked me for six. I was adopted in Canada and brought to England when I was three years of age. During the war I met my brother, who located me, I don't know how. My mother sent me a birthday cable when I was thirty-three, but I never had any wish to see her. I felt my real mother was the person who brought me up and loved me. Your story has proved to me why Coronation Street is top of all the soaps. The story-lines are believable.'

Another viewer wrote, 'May I be permitted to say how much I appreciate the high moral standards displayed in your programme.' But some letters contain brickbats rather than bouquets. Somebody wanted to rap Bet Lynch's knuckles for smoking in the Rovers. Those concerned with the abuse of alcohol would like to see the Rovers pulled down altogether.

In these job-starved days, viewers are quick off the mark to apply for any vacancy in the Street. One wrote, 'Regarding your vacancy in Alf Roberts's corner shop, could you please send me details or an application form as I have considerable experience of stacking shelves and dealing with the general public.' Someone else had his eye on Rita's Kabin. It wasn't a job he wanted but the Kabin itself. 'Could you please forward details, such as takings, rent, rates, lease and accommodation,' he enquired. 'Also, please send a breakdown of sales of different items, i.e.

papers, toys, cards and stationery.' Then there were the three girls who wanted to join Mike Baldwin's workforce. 'We have always worked together since leaving school and would like to continue that way,' they explained.

But perhaps the most unusual letter came to me from a lady who already had the sort of job most people would envy. 'I work as personal assistant to an English millionaire in Monte Carlo, dine at the best hotels, drive the Rolls Royce Corniche and the Lamborghini to commute between my apartment on the Avenue Princess Grace and my employer's villa at Port Grimaud,' the attractive brunette explained in her note, which enclosed an appealing photograph of her relaxing on a sun-kissed balcony. 'My salary is excellent and I have travel expenses, clothes, etc. I should be the happiest woman in the world. But I only see Coronation Street when I have my holiday at my parents' home in Chester.

'I don't suppose you could find me a job like the one I have now somewhere in the world that has Coronation Street on television.'

I pondered her problem for some seconds and recognised an opportunity which was too good to miss. I put pen to paper and told the lady: 'I'm prepared to do a straight swap with you. How are you fixed?'

The Street's Godfather – not ousted in a Mafia-type coup, but following a wish to venture into pastures new

28

MY ABDICATION

The lady from Monte Carlo never did take up the offer. My eventual parting from Coronation Street was much less spectacular, although the press did their best to make it sound dramatic. A couple of years ago when Granada Television adopted a policy to give some of its older employees generous voluntary redundancy, some people, and one tabloid newspaper in particular, put two and two together and made five.

In February 1988 a front-page headline screamed: STREET BOSS GETS THE ELBOW, and went on to declare that in a classic mafia-style operation I had been stripped of my executive producer status during a backstage row over the programme's future and given a £130,000 golden handshake as an offer I couldn't refuse.

The shock of reading the tale was enough to put years on me. But Fleet Street had already done so, since the story described me as a veteran producer aged sixty-one. In fact I was fifty-six, and this was not the only detail in which the story was hopelessly inaccurate. When Granada first made their across-the-board voluntary redundancy offer to all employees over the age of fifty, I simply considered myself far too young to be put out to grass.

A year later, however, after much reflection, I changed my mind and accepted the voluntary redundancy offer

that was still on the table at Granada. I had sat in the producer's chair for thirteen years, a period I have to admit was possibly too long. Coronation Street had consistently topped the ratings for over a decade, but I was far from blind to the fact that someone sitting back with a new and objective view might find areas in which the programme could possibly be improved.

Changes are indeed now taking place. At the time of writing, summer 1989, the Street is heading for possibly the most dramatic shake-up of its history. There is a long-term plan to take Coronation Street into the 1990s, and more than likely the twenty-first century. Spearheading the redesign work is the plan to transmit the serial three times a week. My first question was why? Why interfere so radically with a tremendous success when there is an inherent danger that it could all backfire?

There is a thing called 'overkill' which can never be discounted. I'm quite sure the quality of the programme will remain as high as ever, but had the plan been put to me when I was working on the programme I would have fought against it. I know the cast have mixed feelings about it, and I share some of their misgivings. All I can say at this stage is that, in all sincerity, I hope I'm proved wrong. Three screenings a week will certainly make a good proportion of viewers happy. I regularly received letters asking why the programme couldn't be screened every day of the week. Little did those writers appreciate just how much hard work and creative effort went into making just two episodes.

New houses are to be built along the street and inevitably the cast must grow. It worries me just how many characters the viewers can absorb and care about. The more characters you have, the more each individual is diluted; you can't feature them all at any one time. I thought we had already achieved the optimum balance, and perhaps even tipped the scales slightly on the down side. When I retired the cast numbered almost thirty and was the largest in the programme's history. We would be constantly reminded of the dangers of an expanding cast at the writers' conferences; we had trouble enough creating good story-lines for the characters we had, let alone others we might have liked to introduce. The writers often complained we had too many as it was. To add perhaps another ten will mean that some characters – and possibly firm favourites with the viewers – may not be seen for quite long periods while story-lines float around the others. Transmitting three days a week doesn't mean that more story-lines can be crammed into any one episode. They will simply pass through the programme, and be used up, more speedily.

Coronation Street has never given up the secret of exactly what makes it tick. If that was ever analysed to everyone's satisfaction, it would make all decisions about the programme, including the quite momentous ones being taken now, much easier. During my thirteen years I have managed to come up with a definition of what made the programme such a hit. The secret is simply that – it is a

secret. If I had found the solution I would have bottled it, and be selling the formula for chart-topping soap dramas the world over.

I recall the late Arthur Lowe, talking to me one day about Dad's Army, saying how rare it was for all the ingredients of a television show to come right. When cast, writers, situation, setting and timing all come together, success is reasonably assured. But despite the hard work injected into every programme, it often gels only by sheer chance. Television is littered with the debris of programmes which appeared to have everything going for them but didn't quite turn on the magic.

Coronation Street came together from the first moment and although we can recognise the brilliance of the original casting and writing, there is still an element of its success which no one has put their finger on. Perhaps it is best left in the lap of the gods.

Even while Coronation Street was topping the charts, I experienced a failure when I sidestepped its day-to-day running for a period to become executive producer of a second Granada soap drama, Albion Market. Its eventual demise was very sad. The show didn't do particularly well in ratings at first, so that some Southern ITV companies rescheduled their screenings from good viewing times to not-so-good ones. Changes to the programme had been made and, it seemed to me, we had a formula for success, but it was too late. The decision had been made to axe the programme.

Had it been a BBC programme I can't help feeling it would still be on the air. The BBC are fortunate in that, unlike a commercial company, they don't have to negotiate with all the other independent companies before a programme can be networked. When its Programme Controller makes a decision he doesn't have to talk to five or six other controllers first, nor is he likely to experience great problems caused by northern versus southern interests. The BBC also tend to persevere longer with programmes; a new BBC comedy series, for instance, doesn't run for only seven or thirteen weeks. BBC comedies always have long runs, and those that become most popular are often not great hits in the first place. Dad's Army was a classic example. The first twelve episodes were not even in the top ten of the ratings, but when the series was repeated it went straight to number one. Now that's being brave. The ITV companies tend to be a little more cautious.

But back to Coronation Street. I think there were some in the building – my successor, Mervyn Watson, in particular – who wondered whether I would ever leave at all. Although December 31st was chosen for my official retirement, I had every excuse to be calling into Granada twice or even three times a week long after that and I couldn't resist making the most of it. Mervyn didn't say anything, but I began to get an uneasy feeling that perhaps my face was being seen around the Coronation Street office a little too often. I'm grateful it was tolerated. It made the break so much more gradual, and helped me ease myself out rather than suddenly cutting myself off. Even so it was a great wrench leaving Granada and, of course, especially the Street. After thirteen years I think I could be forgiven for thinking of the show as my baby; I had produced it for almost half its life, and felt I had become a part of it.

When I announced my retirement, rumours of who would be my successor were rife. Mervyn Watson was the obvious choice, since he regularly stood in for me as producer. But before his name was officially announced, many among the cast and production team debated whether the appointment would come from outside or within. And Mervyn took a bit of persuading. He had been successfully making drama series and, just as I had done before I was talked into taking over the Street, he enjoyed the regular prospect of taking on new challenges. Coronation Street is never quite for keeps, but it does require a producer's commitment for at least a year, preferably more. It takes a few months just to get into the swing of the programme. I couldn't resist pointing out to Mervyn that if he stayed in the chair as long as I had he would still be there in the year 2002. He went a paler shade of white.

There were some December mornings at the end of 1988 when I must have looked a similar colour, but not through any portent of the future. My visual appearance was simply the aftermath of the night before. The farewell parties began in early December and somehow seemed to go on into Christmas and the New Year. Thankfully Mervyn had already assumed virtually full responsibility for the programme, so I could relax and thoroughly enjoy what seemed to develop into a very long goodbye.

Coronation Street's annual party is always held on the Friday nearest December 9th, the date of the first transmission. In 1988, the event became my personal leaving party rather than a birthday celebration. Bill Roache made a speech on behalf of the cast and Adele Rose spoke on behalf of the writers. It was all very moving and for me quite emotional. I wasn't going to miss the hard work and day-to-day regime of producing Coronation Street week in

Bill Podmore's retirement party

and week out, year after year. But I was leaving some dear people and great friends behind.

Officially, Granada said farewell at a party for over a hundred guests in the recently refurbished bonded warehouse which adjoins the studio's main administration building. On the night, the entrance was dominated by a shroud which carefully revealed the snout of a very racy TVR sports car. Everyone assumed that someone had gone mad with the company cheque book and there were plans afoot to drive me off the premises in style.

Together with David Plowright, who had organised my last official supper, I knew different. He made a wonderful farewell speech at the end of which a rope was pulled and the gleaming sports car was revealed as bonnetless and missing an engine.

In its place was a rather splendid lawnmower. It was a GT model, of course, the very gift I had chosen for myself and one which I thought would be most useful for someone whose retirement was never planned to last more than one summer.

INDEX

Italics appear for *entries* for fictional characters and places; and for *references to pages* with photographs: e.g. *Armitage, Shirley 152*